Duncan S. Walker

Celebration of the One Hundredth Anniversary of the Laying of the Corner Stone of the Capitol of the United States

Duncan S. Walker

Celebration of the One Hundredth Anniversary of the Laying of the Corner Stone of the Capitol of the United States

ISBN/EAN: 9783337814076

Printed in Europe, USA, Canada, Australia, Japan.

Cover: Foto ©Suzi / pixelio.de

More available books at **www.hansebooks.com**

1793 = = = = 1893

Celebration

OF THE

One Hundredth Anniversary

OF THE

Laying of the Corner Stone

OF THE

Capitol of the United States

With Accounts of the Laying of the Original Corner
Stone, in 1793, and of the Corner Stone
of the Extension, in 1851

General Duncan S. Walker

Editor and Compiler

—

WASHINGTON
GOVERNMENT PRINTING OFFICE
1896

Contents

4 Capitol Centennial Celebration

List of Illustrations

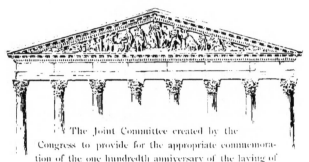

The Joint Committee created by the Congress to provide for the appropriate commemoration of the one hundredth anniversary of the laying of the corner stone of the Capitol of the United States (see page 103) organized with Senator DANIEL W. VOORHEES as Chairman and General DUNCAN S. WALKER as Secretary. The plan and scope of the commemoration were agreed upon substantially as set forth in the accompanying description of the proceedings of the day, and the proper execution of the same was intrusted to the Committee of Citizens, by whom voluntary contributions sufficient to defray the expense of an appropriate celebration of the anniversary were secured, subject to such directions and control as might be deemed necessary by the Joint Committee of Congress.

The official programme of the ceremonies included a civic and military parade over the route taken by the procession on September 18, 1793; prayer by the Right Reverend WILLIAM PARET, Bishop of Maryland; introduction by the Chairman of the Citizens' Committee of the Chairman of Ceremonies, GROVER CLEVELAND, President of the United States; address by President CLEVELAND; oration by WILLIAM WIRT HENRY, of Virginia; address, "The United States Senate," by ADLAI EWING STEVENSON, Vice-President of the United States; address, "The United States House of Representatives," by CHARLES FREDERICK CRISP, Speaker of the House; address, "The Judiciary," by Mr. Justice HENRY BILLINGS BROWN, United States Supreme Court; address, "The District of Columbia," by MYRON M. PARKER, Commissioner of the District of Columbia. The vocal music was rendered by a trained "Centennial Chorus" of fifteen hundred adult voices, and the instrumental music by the United States Marine Band.

In the evening there was an appropriate illumination of the east front of the Capitol building and a concert by the Centennial Chorus and the Marine Band.

The programme agreed upon by the Joint Committee was faithfully adhered to, and without any expense whatever to the United States Government.

A full description of the proceedings of the day; a history of the legislation of Congress providing for the celebration, for the erection of a tablet to mark the corner stone, and for the publication of the proceedings of the day; minutes of the meetings of the Joint Committee of Congress, and an account of the organization and proceedings of the Citizens' Committee are included. It was thought appropriate also to add the best accounts obtainable of the ceremonies attending the laying of the corner stone of the original Capitol building, September 18, 1793, and of the corner stone of the extension of the Capitol, July 4, 1851, and a condensed history of the Capitol building, with a brief sketch of the architects engaged at different times in its construction and care.

Organization and Work

Organization and Work

THE MOVEMENT for the commemoration of the centennial anniversary of the laying of the corner stone of the Nation's Capitol was initiated by a motion made by Mr. M. I. WELLER at a meeting of the East Washington Citizens' Association, September 3, 1891. The motion was agreed to, and the Association requested appropriate action by the Board of Commissioners of the District of Columbia. Accordingly a call was issued by the Commissioners for a public meeting, which was held on June 7, 1893. Hon. JOHN W. ROSS, President of the Board of Commissioners, presided, and selected a committee of fifty citizens to conduct the preparations for the celebration. This General Committee was composed and officered as follows:

GENERAL COMMITTEE

[In charge of all matters pertaining to the celebration, with power to appoint such officers, agents, and subcommittees as may be necessary.]

LAWRENCE GARDNER, *Chairman.*
C. C. GLOVER, *Vice-Chairman.*
EDWIN B. HAY, *Secretary.*
M. I. WELLER, *Corresponding Secretary.*
S. W. WOODWARD, *Treasurer.*

J. W. BABSON.	J. J. DARLINGTON.	GEORGE T. DUNLOP.
H. L. BISCOE.	MILLS DEAN.	J. J. EDSON.
H. V. BOYNTON.	HARRISON DINGMAN	W. J. FRIZZELL.
A. T. BRITTON.	W. C. DODGE.	WILLIAM A. GORDON

11

O. C. GREEN.
H. A. GRISWOLD.
JULES GUTHRIDGE.
E. J. HANNAN.
CHRIS. HEURICH.
J. HARRISON JOHNSON.
F. A. LEHMAN.
THOMAS F. MILLER.
F. L. MOORE.
THEODORE W. NOYES.
M. M. PARKER.

CHARLES F. POWELL.
JOHN W. ROSS.
SAMUEL ROSS.
ISADORE SAKS.
JAMES F. SCAGGS.
HENRY SHERWOOD.
THOMAS SOMERVILLE.
A. R. SPOFFORD.
THOMAS W. SMITH.
ELLIS SPEAR.
A. F. SPERRY.

W. J. STEPHENSON.
Dr. J. M. TONER.
SEYMOUR W. TULLOCH.
DUNCAN S. WALKER.
B. H. WARNER.
J. W. WHELPLEY.
BERIAH WILKINS.
L. C. WILLIAMSON.
L. D. WINE.
MARSHALL W. WINES.
S. S. YODER.

SUBCOMMITTEES

As the work of preparation progressed it was found necessary to
appoint the following subcommittees and to define their duties:

INVITATION COMMITTEE

[Under the direction of the General Committee, to prepare suitable invitations and issue the
same to distinguished guests.]

Gen. DUNCAN S. WALKER, *Chairman.*
Gen. H. V. BOYNTON, *Vice-Chairman.*
MARSHALL W. WINES, *Secretary.*

Commissioner JOHN W. ROSS.
Commissioner M. M. PARKER.
Commissioner CHARLES F. POWELL.
Chief Justice M. W. FULLER.
Hon. EPPA HUNTON.

Hon. BARNES COMPTON.
Judge M. F. MORRIS.
Prof. J. C. WELLING.
FRANK HATTON.
THEO. W. NOYES.

CEREMONIES AT CAPITOL COMMITTEE

[In charge of formulating a plan and determining all ceremonies and exercises at the Capitol,
except exercises in charge of the Evening Entertainment Committee.]

B. H. WARNER, *Chairman.*
A. R. SPOFFORD, *Vice-Chairman.*

CHARLES C. GLOVER.
Dr. JOSEPH M. TONER.
J. W. WHELPLEY.

J. J. DARLINGTON.
EDWARD CLARK.
MILLS DEAN.

COMMITTEE ON SCOPE

[In charge of all matters pertaining to the celebration, such as determining the character of
celebration, what committees are necessary, and their numbers.]

J. W. BABSON, *Chairman.*

Dr. JOSEPH M. TONER.
M. I. WELLER.
W. J. STEPHENSON.

MILLS DEAN.
F. L. MOORE.
HENRY SHERWOOD.

COMMITTEE ON LEGISLATION

[To prepare and obtain necessary legislation approved by the General Committee]

LAWRENCE GARDNER, *Chairman.*

Gen. DUNCAN S. WALKER.   Dr. JOSEPH M. TONER.

RECEPTION COMMITTEE

[To receive and extend proper courtesies to distinguished guests]

BERIAH WILKINS, *Chairman.*

Dr. WILLIAM TINDALL, *Secretary.*

Members of the General Committee

Ex-Governor A. R. SHEPHERD.

Ex-Mayor JAMES G. BERRET.	Ex-Commissioner WILLIAM B. WEBB.
Ex-Mayor M. G. EMERY.	Ex-Commissioner S. E. WHEATLEY.
Ex-Mayor SAYLES J. BOWEN.	Ex-Commissioner J. W. DOUGLASS.
Ex-Commissioner JOHN H. KETCHAM.	Ex-Commissioner L. G. HINE.
Ex-Commissioner THOMAS B. BRYAN.	Ex-Commissioner G. J. LYDECKER.
Ex-Commissioner J. DENT.	Ex-Commissioner WILLIAM LUDLOW.
Ex-Commissioner T. P. MORGAN.	Ex-Commissioner C. W. RAYMOND.
Ex-Commissioner J. R. WEST.	Ex-Commissioner H. M. ROBERT.
Ex-Commissioner J. B. EDMONDS.	Ex-Commissioner WILLIAM T. ROSSELL.

Gen. NICHOLAS ANDERSON.	Dr. W. W. GODDING.	A. P. MORSE.
MAHLON B. ASHFORD.	G. CLAY GOODLOE.	D. I. MURPHY.
CHARLES B. BAILEY.	GEORGE C. GORHAM.	CLARENCE F. NORMENT.
JOHN A. BAKER.	JOHN T. GIVEN.	N. G. ORDWAY.
JAMES L. BARBOUR.	WILLIAM B. GURLEY.	GEORGE M. OYSTER.
L. J. BATES.	Col. JOHN HAY.	ANTHONY POLLOCK.
C. J. BELL.	Gen. S. S. HENKLE.	GEORGE R. REPETTI.
M. W. BEVERIDGE.	Col. CHARLES HEYWOOD.	F. A. RICHARDSON.
Gen. WILLIAM BIRNEY.	WILLIAM C. HILL.	E. FRANCIS RIGGS.
CHAPIN BROWN.	CURTIS J. HILLYER.	BUSHROD ROBINSON.
N. W. BURCHELL.	W. S. HOGE.	THEO. ROESSLE.
Gen. CYRUS BUSSEY.	ROBERT O. HOLTZMAN.	WILLIAM H. SELDEN.
JOHN L. CARROLL.	GARDNER G. HUBBARD.	H. W. SOHON.
H. H. CARTER.	FRANK HUME.	JAMES W. SOMERVILLE.
EUGENE CARUSI.	STILSON HUTCHINS.	O. G. STAPLES.
JOHN CASSELLS.	Maj. W. P. HUXFORD.	E. J. STELLWAGEN.
GEORGE W. COCHRAN.	JAMES KERR.	JOHN A. SWOPE.
H. L. CRANFORD.	T. A. LAMBERT.	H. T. TAGGART.
WILLIAM S. CROSBY.	L. Z. LEITER.	A. A. THOMAS.
WASH. DANENHOWER.	GEORGE E. LEMON.	S. T. THOMAS.
WALTER D. DAVIDGE.	A. A. LIPSCOMB.	HENRY T. THURBER.
HENRY E. DAVIS.	DANIEL LOUGHRAN.	ENOCH TOTTEN.
JOHN T. DEVINE.	SAMUEL MADDOX.	H. O. TOWLES.
J. MAURY DOVE.	Dr. THOMAS F. MALLAN.	THOMAS E. WAGGAMAN.
CHARLES C. DUNCANSON.	M. MAREAN.	CHARLES E. WHITE.
JAMES S. EDMONDS.	Dr. WILLIAM V. MARMION.	C. C. WILLARD.
W. E. EDMONSTON.	C. M. MATTHEWS.	H. A. WILLARD.
J. C. ERGOOD.	WILLIAM F. MATTINGLY.	WASH. B. WILLIAMS.
Capt. G. J. FIEBEGER.	F. B. McGUIRE.	Col. J. M. WILSON.
ALBERT F. FOX.	W. CRANCH McINTYRE.	LEVI WOODBURY.
Dr. EDW. M. GALLAUDET.	D. P. McKEEVER.	SIMON WOLF.
H. WISE GARNETT.	JOHN R. McLEAN.	A. S. WORTHINGTON.

COMMITTEE ON PUBLIC ORDER AND COMFORT

[To cooperate with the District authorities in securing the necessary aid for enforcing the requisite regulations and to clear the avenue and streets for the formation and movement of the procession. Also authorized to consult with the proper authorities in charge of the United States Capitol for the preservation of order in the Capitol grounds and such other matters as in their judgment may be necessary for the protection and comfort of the public, both during the ceremonies and evening entertainment.]

HENRY L. BISCOE, *Chairman*,

W. L. CASH.	M. A. McGOWAN.
W. B. EASTON.	Col. W. G. MOORE.
GEORGE H. GADDES.	JOSEPH PARRIS.
JOHN KENWORTH.	THOMAS A. ROVER.
A. W. KELLEY.	H. L. STREET.
J. FRED. KELLY.	RICHARD SYLVESTER.
NOBLE D. LARNER.	J. P. WRIGHT.

EVENING ENTERTAINMENT COMMITTEE

[Charged with all matters pertaining to the evening ceremonies except illumination of the Capitol and fireworks.]

JULES GUTHRIDGE, *Chairman*.
A. T. BRITTON, *Vice-Chairman*.
JAMES F. SCAGGS, *Secretary*.

JOB BARNARD.	JAMES LANSBURGH.
A. M. BLISS.	W. A. McKENNY.
ROBERT CHRISTIE.	THOMAS F. MILLER.
HARRISON DINGMAN.	E. A. MOSELEY.
GEORGE T. DUNLOP.	R. ROSS PERRY.
REGINALD FENDALL.	RICHARD SMITH.
H. W. GARNETT.	S. W. TULLOCH.
O. C. GREEN.	Gen. THOMAS M. VINCENT.
GEORGE E. HAMILTON.	L. C. WILLIAMSON.

LOUIS D. WINE.

RAILROAD RATES COMMITTEE

[To obtain the lowest possible railroad rates from all points in the Union to this city, and announce the same to the public as fast as received.]

THOMAS W. SMITH, *Chairman*.

E. W. ANDERSON.	SAMUEL ROSS.
H. L. BISCOE.	W. J. STEPHENSON.

COMMITTEE ON STANDS

[In charge of the erection and decorating of a stand in front of the Capitol and such other stands as the Executive Committee shall order.]

WILLIAM J. FRIZZELL, *Chairman*.

HARRY BARTON.	T. L. HOLBROOK.
OWEN DONNELLY.	H. F. HOLSTEN.
WILLIAM HOLMEAD.	C. C. MEADS.

CAPITOL DECORATION COMMITTEE

[In charge of the decoration of the Capitol and the approaches thereto.]

S. S. YODER, *Chairman.*

R. B. BUCKLEY.
JOHN R. CARMODY.
THOMAS N. CONRAD.
C. H. FICKLING.
BENJAMIN F. GUY.
CHARLES H. HARRIS.
E. J. HANNAN.

J. J. S. HASSLER.
JAMES F. HOOD.
TRACY L. JEFFORDS.
JAMES D. MAHER.
GEORGE W. MOSS.
W. H. RUPP.
GEORGE W. TALBERT.

J. H. C. WILSON.

MUSIC COMMITTEE

[Charged with the duty of engaging the necessary music for the celebration, subject to the approval of the Executive Committee.]

WILLIAM A. GORDON, *Chairman.*
Dr. FRANK T. HOWE, *Chairman Subcommittee on Chorus.*
RALPH L. GALT, *Chairman Subcommittee on Band.*

A. B. COPPES.
JAMES H. FORSYTH.
FRED. A. GRANT.
J. E. JONES.
WILLIAM H. MANOGUE.

JOHN A. ROEDER.
W. A. SLACK.
JOSEPH I. WELLER.
JAMES P. WILLETT.
LEONARD C. WOOD.

S. M. YEATMAN.

PRINTING COMMITTEE

[To supervise such printing as may be referred to them and ordered by the Executive Committee. Also in charge of any designing and printing or publications that may be authorized by the Executive Committee.]

A. F. SPERRY, *Chairman.*

ARTHUR ST. C. DENVER.
GEORGE H. HARRIES.

DAVID MOORE.
WILLIAM H. RAPLEY.

BADGES AND SOUVENIR MEDALS COMMITTEE

[To cause designs for badges and souvenir medals and the cost thereof to be submitted for the approval of the Executive Committee, and when so authorized to secure and deliver the same to the chairman of the Executive Committee.]

THOMAS SOMERVILLE, *Chairman.*

GEORGE W. CASILEAR.
D. I. MURPHY.
SIDNEY H. NEALEY.

H. H. TWOMBLY.
JOSEPH WALTMEYER.
GEORGE GIBSON.

PRESS COMMITTEE

[To arrange for the accommodation of the press and to extend all necessary facilities.]

THEODORE W. NOYES, *Chairman.*
P. V. DE GRAW, *Vice-Chairman.*
HENRY L. WEST, *Secretary.*

GEORGE W. ABELL.	E. G. DUNNELL.	FRANK P. MORGAN.
FELIX AGNUS.	W. H. DENNIS.	FRANK J. O'NEILL.
THOMAS G. ALVORD.	J. HADLEY DOYLE.	JOHN H. ROCHE.
ALEX. D. ANDERSON.	FERGUS P. FERRIS.	MAURICE SPLAIN.
ADDISON B. ATKINS.	HARRY P. GODWIN.	JOHN G. SLATER.
EDWARD W. BARRETT.	GEORGE H. HARRIES.	HAROLD SNOWDEN.
DAVID S. BARRY.	FRANK H. HOSFORD.	ORLANDO O. STEALEY.
C. C. BOWSFIELD.	THOMAS B. KALBFUS.	ALFRED J. STOFER.
JOHN BOYLE.	RUDOLPH KAUFFMANN.	LOUIS SCHADE.
HOBART BROOKS.	S. H. KAUFFMANN.	R. H. SYLVESTER.
LOGAN CARLISLE.	HORACE KENNEY.	JOHN TRACEY.
CHARLES C. CARLTON.	R. M. LARNER.	CLIFFORD WARDEN.
JOHN M. CARSON.	FRANCIS E. LEUPP.	WALTER WELLMAN.
CLUSKEY CROMWELL.	A. MAURICE LOWE.	E. B. WIGHT.
WILLIAM L. CROUNSE.	R. BOWMAN MATTHEWS.	R. J. WYNNE.
MARSHALL CUSHING.	JOHN P. MILLER.	
R. H. DARBY.	O'BRIEN MOORE.	

PARADE COMMITTEE

[In charge of all matters pertaining to parade, both civic and military, organize the same, and at the proper time turn it over to the Grand Marshal.]

Gen. ELLIS SPEAR, *Chairman.*
CHARLES W. DARR, *Vice-Chairman.*

ROBERT BALL.	DANIEL FRAZIER.
Capt. HARRISON BARBOUR.	GEORGE GIBSON.
ROBERT BOYD.	Col. C. HEYWOOD, U. S. M. C.
Lieut. Col. HARRY COGGIN.	Capt. JOSEPH O. MANSON.
Capt. C. S. DOMER.	Capt. JOHN S. MILLER.
S. E. FAUNCE.	Capt. ALLISON NAILOR.

JOHN J. PEABODY.

ILLUMINATION COMMITTEE

[In charge of illuminating the Capitol and matters pertaining to illumination and fireworks.]

FRED. A. LEHMAN, *Chairman.*
WILLIAM F. HART, *Vice-Chairman.*
A. W. HART, *Secretary.*
A. B. CLAXTON, *Chairman Subcommittee on Fireworks.*

GUSTAV BISSING.	C. P. GLEIM.
ALBERT BRIGHT.	O. B. HALLAM.
EDWARD CLARK.	WILLIAM McADOO.
Capt. GEORGE McC. DERBY.	B. N. MORRIS.
Capt. G. J. FIEBEGER.	GEORGE L. MORTON.
MAX GEORGII.	A. S. PATTISON.

A. R. TOWNSEND.

FINANCE COMMITTEE

[Charged with raising funds for the expenses of the celebration. When collected, to be paid over to the treasurer by the chairman.]

JOHN JOY EDSON, *Chairman.*
FRANK P. REESIDE, *Secretary.*

ANDREW ARCHER.
JOHN T. ARMS.
BRENT. L. BALDWIN.
W. B. BALDWIN.
W. D. BALDWIN.
F. H. BARBARIN.
JAMES L. BARBOUR.
JOB BARNARD.
HARRY BARTON.
CHARLES J. BELL.
H. H. BERGMAN.
E. P. BERRY.
SAMUEL BIEBER.
J. WESLEY BOTELER.
CHARLES C. BRADLEY.
S. THOMAS BROWN.
HORATIO BROWNING.
HENRY C. BURCH.
ALBERT CARRY.
J. W. CHAPPELL.
DANIEL B. CLARK.
WILLIAM E. CLARK.
DENNIS CONNELL.
CLARENCE CORSON.
SAMUEL CROSS.
SAMUEL W. CURRIDEN.
C. H. DAVIDGE.
LOUIS J. DAVIS.
GEORGE W. DRIVER.
EDWARD F. DROOP.
C. C. DUNCANSON.
W. CLARENCE DUVALL.
S. G. EBERLY.
JOHN C. ECKLOFF.
MATTHEW G. EMERY.
GEORGE E. EMMONS.
A. P. FARDON.
C. H. FICKLING.
Dr. GEORGE W. FISHER.
JAMES E. FITCH.
Prof. W. G. FOWLER.
WILLIAM J. FRIZZELL.
ANDREW GLEASON.
J. H. GORDON.
THOMAS GRAY.
A. M. GREEN.

H. A. GRISWOLD.
CHARLES E. GROSS.
WILLIAM B. GURLEY.
JULES GUTHRIDGE.
GEORGE F. HARBIN.
WALTER HEISTON.
GEORGE C. HENNING.
JOHN E. HERRELL.
D. P. HICKLING.
THEO. L. HOLBROOK.
A. H. F. HOLSTEN.
R. O. HOLTZMAN.
C. W. HOWARD.
CHARLES A. JAMES.
A. S. JOHNSON.
J. B. JOHNSON.
J. HARRISON JOHNSON.
GEORGE A. JORDON.
JOHN G. JUDD.
ARTHUR L. KEANE.
GEORGE KILLEEN.
GEORGE H. KENNEDY.
J. J. KLEINER.
T. A. LAMBERT.
JAMES LANSBURGH.
JOHN B. LARNER.
F. A. LEHMAN.
B. F. LEIGHTON.
GEORGE E. LEMON.
L. A. LITTLEFIELD.
PHILO J. LOCKWOOD.
MEYER LOEB.
A. M. LOTHROP.
JOHN W. MACARTY.
FRANK P. MADIGAN.
JOHN H. MAGRUDER.
WILLIAM H. MANOGUE.
CLARENCE McCLELLAND.
W. W. McCULLOUGH.
A. M. McLACHLEN.
FRANK B. MOHUN.
W. C. MORRISON.
ALLISON NAILOR, Jr.
FRANK P. NOYES.
GEORGE M. OYSTER.
JAMES F. OYSTER.

E. S. PARKER.
JOHN C. PARKER.
THOMAS C. PEARSALL.
SEATON PERRY.
EUGENE PETERS.
J. T. PETTY.
W. W. RAPLEY.
FRANK T. RAWLINGS.
E. FRANCIS RIGGS.
T. E. ROESSLE.
SAMUEL ROSS.
A. B. RUFF.
ISADORE SAKS.
Dr. A. J. SCHAFHIRT.
JOHN W. SHAFER.
SAMUEL S. SHEDD.
JOHN G. SLATER.
THOMAS W. SMITH.
B. F. SNYDER.
THOMAS SOMERVILLE.
O. G. STAPLES.
E. J. STELLWAGEN.
FREDERICK C. STEVENS.
F. A. STIER.
A. L. STURTEVANT.
J. S. SWORMSTED.
GEORGE W. TALBERT.
JOSEPH D. TAYLOR.
A. A. THOMAS.
JOHN W. THOMPSON.
O. T. THOMPSON.
W. S. THOMPSON.
LEM. TOWERS, Jr.
R. A. WALKER.
SAMUEL H. WALKER.
B. H. WARNER.
JOHN L. WEAVER.
EDWARD S. WESCOTT.
FRANK P. WELLER.
W. J. WHELPLEY.
CHARLES E. WHITE.
GEORGE H. B. WHITE.
BERIAH WILKINS.
CHARLES P. WILLIAMS.
JESSE B. WILSON.
LOUIS D. WINE.

H. Mis. 211——2

AUDITING COMMITTEE

[All bills must be examined by the committee, to ascertain if they have been properly authorized by the Executive Committee by order or by appropriation, and approved by the chairman of the Executive Committee. When so examined and approved by the chairman of the Committee on Auditing, the Treasurer shall draw his check for the amount of the bills, which shall then be paid. All statements or reports made up by the Executive Committee of receipts and disbursements must be verified and approved by the Committee on Auditing.]

ISADORE SAKS, *Chairman.*

GEORGE C. HENNING.   CLEM. W. HOWARD.

STREET DECORATION COMMITTEE

Charged with the duty of securing decorations for and decorating the avenues and streets and the national and city government buildings.]

HARRISON DINGMAN, *Chairman.*

REUBEN F. BAKER.	I. W. HOPKINS.
HARRISON BARBOUR.	HARRY R. HOWSER.
ROBERT BEALL.	W. A. HUTCHINS.
HENRY L. BRYAN.	GEORGE W. JOYCE.
ALBERT CARRY.	Prof. HARRY KING.
S. W. CURRIDEN.	C. C. LANCASTER.
WILLIAM DICKSON.	FRANK P. MADDGAN.
EDWIN F. DROOP.	EDWARD MINNIX.
J. H. GORDON.	F. S. PARKS.
WM. HOEKE.	GEORGE F. PYLES.

OFFICERS OF THE PARADE

The following officers of the parade were appointed:

Grand Marshal: Gen. ALBERT ORDWAY.
Chief of Staff: Gen. ELLIS SPEAR.
Special Aids: Col. H. C. CORBIN. U. S. A.
                 Capt. GEORGE P. SCHRIVER, U. S. A.

Aids

ARTHUR D. ANDERSON.	EUGENE B. CARUSI.	J. MAURY DOVE.
E. W. ANDERSON.	THORNTON A. CARUSI.	J. HADLEY DOYLE.
T. H. ANDERSON.	DORSEY CLAGGETT.	LANIER DUNN.
JOSEPH L. ATKINS.	BARNES COMPTON, Jr.	JOHN JOY EDSON, Jr.
ROBERT BALL.	JOHN T. CROWLEY.	Maj. THOMAS M. GALE.
RALPH BARNARD.	A. J. CURTIS.	ARTHUR P. GORMAN, Jr.
J. A. BARTHEL.	ST. JULIAN DAPRAY.	Dr. W. HAMMETT.
N. BESTOR.	CHARLES W. DARR.	Maj. WILLIAM HARMER.
E. H. BLOCK.	WALTER D. DAVIDGE, Jr.	ROBERT HARROVER.
LEE BRITTON.	WILLIAM W. DEANE.	F. J. HART.
Capt. WILLIAM BROWN.	Gen. J. DICKINSON.	RICHARD K. HARVEY.
S. S. BURDETT.	WILLIAM DICKSON.	WILLIAM B. HIBBS.
Maj. F. A. BUTTS.	J. FRANKLIN DONOHUE.	S. HODGKINS.

Robert O. Holtzman.	James J. McDonald.	John J. Repetti.
Frank Hume, Jr.	George X. McLanahan.	Leigh Robinson.
Maj. T. W. Hungerford.	W. H. Michael.	I. N. Runyan.
Maj. Robert W. Hunter.	Maj. Julian G. Moore.	Col. J. H. Strickland.
Capt. J. H. Johnson.	Maj. A. Porter Morse.	Magnus S. Thompson.
Prof. J. Harry King.	H. C. Moses.	Julius W. Tolson.
Thomas J. King.	Washington Nailor.	Maj. E. B. Townsend.
S. Prentiss Knott.	Edward G. Niles.	John Tweedale.
Blair Lee.	James L. Norris, Jr.	H. H. Twombly.
L. A. Littlefield.	Gen. J. N. Patterson.	Hugh Waddell.
Woodbury Lowery, Jr.	George H. Penrose.	Albert C. Walker.
Dr. J. Maloney.	H. L. Prince.	Joseph I. Weller.
William H. Manogue.	George W. Rae.	Dr. William P. Young.
Col. T. R. Marshall.	J. B. Randolph.	W. H. Zimmerman.

SCOPE OF THE CELEBRATION

The plans for the celebration were all prepared by the Citizens' Committee, and, upon approval by the Joint Committee appointed under the joint resolution of Congress, were carried into execution by the Citizens' Committee.

From the very beginning the Citizens' Committee recognized that the event to be celebrated was of great national importance, and, as soon as the Congress assembled in extra session, submitted the matter to the Vice-President of the United States and to the Speaker of the House of Representatives. The Congress immediately acted, and passed a joint resolution (see p. 102) providing for a committee of fourteen, to consist of seven Senators and seven Representatives, to act with a similar number of citizens to be selected by the Citizens' Committee, "to take order in the matter of arranging for the ceremonies at the Capitol."

THE JOINT COMMITTEE

The Joint Committee was composed and officered as follows:

Chairman: Hon. Daniel Wolsey Voorhees, United States Senate.
Secretary: Gen. Duncan S. Walker.

Senators

Daniel W. Voorhees.	John Sherman.
Matt W. Ransom.	Stephen M. White.
William E. Chandler.	Watson C. Squire.
John Martin.	

Representatives

WILLIAM D. BYNUM.	JOHN C. BLACK.
DAVID B. HENDERSON.	JOHN DE WITT WARNER.
GEORGE W. HOUK.	CHARLES O'NEILL.
	WILLIAM COGSWELL.

Citizens

LAWRENCE GARDNER.	MICHAEL I. WELLER.
Gen. DUNCAN S. WALKER.	E. B. HAY.
C. C. GLOVER.	S. W. WOODWARD.
JOHN W. ROSS.	H. L. BISCOE.
B. H. WARNER.	A. R. SPOFFORD.
J. M. TONER.	JOHN JOY EDSON.
BERIAH WILKINS.	MARSHALL W. WINES.

At meetings of the Joint Committee the plans for the celebration drawn up by the Citizens' Committee were approved and directed to be carried into effect (see pp. 92–95).

LEGISLATION BY CONGRESS

It was also agreed by the Joint Committee that Congress should be requested to make the 18th day of September, 1893, a legal holiday within the District of Columbia, and to lend certain army and navy flags to the Architect of the Capitol for decorative purposes, and that the Senate and the House of Representatives be invited to attend the exercises at the Capitol. Congress responded favorably to the requests and accepted the invitation (see pp. 95, 103–106).

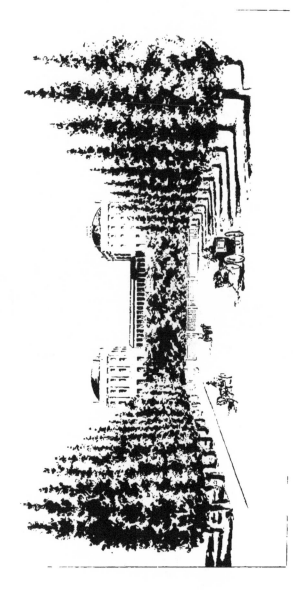

The Programme

Official Programme

The following is the official programme for the celebration agreed upon and executed:

CONCERTS BY CENTENNIAL CHIMES

From 9 to 10 a. m.

1. National peal, changes rung on thirteen bells.
2. America (My Country, 'Tis of Thee).
3. Ring Out, Wild Bells. (Mrs. Abby Hutchinson Patton.)
4. Old Coronation.
5. The Sweet By and By.
6. Blue Bells of Scotland.
7. The British Grenadiers.
8. The Bells of Shandon.
9. Maryland, My Maryland.
10. De Bériot's Fifth Air.
11. Way Down upon the Suwannee River.
12. Schubert's Ave Maria.
13. Columbia, the Gem of the Ocean.
14. Oft in the Stilly Night.
15. Dixie.
16. Old Black Joe.
17. Haste to the Wedding.
18. Massa's in the Cold, Cold Ground.
19. Bonny Doon.
20. What Fairy-like Music.
21. National salute, the thirteen bells being struck in unison forty-four times.

From 1 to 2 p. m.

1. Centennial peal, changes rung on thirteen bells.
2. My Country, 'Tis of Thee (America).
3. The Bells, march. (Battmann.)
4. Robin Adair. (Keppel.)
5. La Marseillaise. (Rouget de l'Isle.)
6. Believe Me, If All Those Endearing Young Charms. (Tom Moore.)
7. Chimes of Corneville. (Planquette.)
8. Rose Marie.
9. Wo ist des Deutchen Vaterland? (Reichardt.)
10. Way Down upon the Suwannee River. (Foster.)
11. (a) Monastery Bells.
    (b) Ave Maria Stella. (Vely.)
12. De Bériot's Fifth Air.

13. Die Kapelle (The Chapel). (Kreutzer.)
14. Guide Me, O Thou Great Jehovah. (Flotow.)
15.   (*a*) Prayer from Zampa. (Herold.)
      (*b*) Wedding March—Lohengrin. (Wagner.)
16. Ring Out, Wild Bells. (Mrs. Abby Hutchinson Patton.)
17. Heimaths-Klänge. (Silcher.)
18. Oft in the Stilly Night. (Moore.)
19. Hear the Music of the Bells.
20. The Sweet By and By.
21. Le Carillon. (Streabog.)
22. Maryland, My Maryland.
23. National salute, change peal, the thirteen bells being struck in unison forty-four times.

ROUTE OF PARADE

The parade to start at 1 p. m. and to arrive at the Capitol before 2 p. m., the line of march (same as on September 18, 1793) to begin on Pennsylvania avenue near Fifteenth street northwest; thence south down Fifteenth street to Pennsylvania avenue; thence down Pennsylvania avenue to the Capitol grounds; thence to B street north; by B street north to First street east, to B street south; thence to New Jersey avenue, there to be dismissed.

EXERCISES AT THE CAPITOL

The following was decided on as the programme at the Capitol, commencing at 2 p. m. :

Music—Overture to Tannhauser..............................Marine Band
Prayer...................Right Reverend WILLIAM PARET, Bishop of Maryland
Music—Te Deum in E flat. (Dudley Buck).......................Grand Chorus
Introduction.............LAWRENCE GARDNER, Chairman of General Committee
Chairman of Ceremonies.....GROVER CLEVELAND, President of the United States
Music—Selections—Lakmé.......................................Marine Band
Orator of the Day...........................WILLIAM WIRT HENRY, Virginia
Music—Star-Spangled Banner....................................Grand Chorus
Address—The United States Senate.........ADLAI E. STEVENSON, Vice-President
Music—Potpourri of national airs.............................Marine Band
Address—The United States House of Representatives...CHARLES F. CRISP, Speaker
Music—The Heavens are Telling (Creation)......................Grand Chorus
Address—The Judiciary...HENRY BILLINGS BROWN, Supreme Court United States
Music—Centennial March. (Fanciulli)..........................Marine Band
Address—The District of Columbia.
            MYRON M. PARKER, Commissioner District of Columbia
Music—America.................Marine Band, Grand Chorus, and audience

The vocal music to be sung by a chorus of fifteen hundred voices, under the direction of Professor N. DU SHANE CLOWARD.

EVENING CONCERT

The Centennial Chimes, from 6 to 7 p. m., to render the numbers following:

1. Change peal on national airs.
2. Rally 'Round the Flag, Boys.
3. Auld Lang Syne.
4. Carry Me Back to Old Virginny. (Foster.)
5. Prayer from Der Freischutz. (Von Weber.)
6. Oh, Summer Night—Don Pasquale.
7. Ave Maria. (Schubert.)
8. Camptown Races. (Christy.)
9. Bonny Blue Flag.
10. Home Again.
11. Robin Adair.
12. De Bériot's Fifth Air.
13. Those Evening Bells. (Tom Moore.)
14. Home, Sweet Home. (Payne.)
15. Old Folks at Home. (Foster.)
16. Nearer, My God, to Thee—Bethany.
17. The Last Rose of Summer. (Moore.)
18. Wedding March—Lohengrin. (Wagner.)
19. Oft in the Stilly Night. (Moore.)
20. Star-Spangled Banner. (Key.)
21. National peal, change salute, all the bells being struck in unison forty-four times.

At the east front of the Capitol, commencing at 8 p. m., the following programme:

1. Grand march—National Capitol Centennial. (Fanciulli).........Marine Band
2. Chorus—The Heavens are Telling (Creation).........Grand Centennial Chorus
3. Overture—Semiramide. (Rossini)...........................Marine Band
4. Home, Sweet Home. (Payne)... ....Centennial Chorus
5. Monastery Bells. (Vely)...............................Marine Band
6. Coronation......................................Centennial Chorus
7. Trip to Manhattan Beach. (Fanciulli)... ....Marine Band
8. Hail Columbia. (Fyles)...........................Centennial Chorus
9. In the Clock Store. (Orth)...........................Marine Band
10. Recitation—The Star-Spangled Banner. (Key).....Mr. CHARLES B. HANFORD
11. Chorus—Star-Spangled Banner...Centennial Chorus, Marine Band, and audience
12. Voyage Comique—A Trip to Mars. (Fanciulli).... ....Marine Band

The chimes of thirteen large bells, from the McShane Foundry, Baltimore, were stationed on the top of the wall at the northwest corner of the new Congressional Library building, and were operated by Professor JOHN R. GIBSON, of the Metropolitan Methodist Episcopal Church, Washington, and Professor PAUL STOFFER, of St. Alphonso Church, Baltimore. The first concert by the chimes began according to programme, at 9 a. m., and continued until nearly 11 o'clock. At 1 p. m. the second concert began, and the evening concert began at 6 o'clock, ending with the "Star-Spangled Banner" and the "National Peal," a change salute, all the thirteen bells being rung in unison forty-four times.

The vocal music rendered during the afternoon and in the evening at the Capitol was by the Grand Centennial Chorus, of fifteen hundred adult voices, conducted by Professor N. DU SHANE CLOWARD. Several weeks preceding the event Professor CLOWARD had divided the District into subdivisions and trained the subdivisions separately, having one grand rehearsal of fifteen hundred voices at Convention Hall on the evening of September 13, 1893.

The United States Marine Band, Professor FANCIULLI conductor, rendered the instrumental music, both at the afternoon exercises and at the evening concert at the Capitol, and accompanied the Centennial Chorus on those occasions.

DECORATIONS AND ILLUMINATION

The principal decorations at the Capitol were upon the central portion of the east front. The grand stands, extending from the north to the south wing, or over the whole east front of the main building and old wings, were draped with bunting, extending back to the cornice, while the front of the stands was hung with

American flags, gracefully caught up at regular intervals with red, white, and blue rosettes. A white anchor on a background of blue covered the center of the main stand, from which the orations were delivered. High upon the center of the main building were hung two large garrison flags, from which was suspended the national coat of arms. Higher up still, on the top of the great white dome, four large American flags floated from horizontal staffs, pointing north, south, east, and west.

With the double purpose of illuminating the east front of the Capitol and furnishing light for the evening concert, at each corner of the central stand was placed a spray of twenty-four colored globes. Between the columns of the main portico were arches of lighted jets, and bands of jets incased in globes encircled the massive pillars. To the right of the grand central stairway, in near proximity to the corner stone of the Capitol, was a large gilded framework, illuminated by jets in globes, reading "1793—WASHINGTON," while to the left of the central stairway a similar illumination read, "1893—CLEVELAND."

GRAND STANDS

There were three grand stands erected at the east front of the Capitol. The central one, for the President, the orators of the day, the Cabinet and other executive officers, the Judiciary, the Diplomatic Corps, and other distinguished guests, covered the whole space of the center of the main building and adjoined the rotunda, from which was the main entrance for the guests, the orators entering from the southeast front of the platform. The capacity of this stand exceeded twenty-five hundred. To the north of this stand and adjoining it was the stand for the Senate and House, under the control of the Sergeants-at-Arms of those bodies, with a seating capacity of fifteen hundred. To the south of the main stand and adjoining it was the grand stand for the Centennial Chorus, with a seating capacity of sixteen hundred, and facing it were the accommodations for the Marine Band. All of these stands were tastefully decorated, as before described.

STREET DECORATIONS

The decorations on the private buildings on Pennsylvania avenue, from the Capitol to the White House, were profuse and beautiful. From every window on each side of the street large flags and strips of bunting were streaming, while many buildings were topped with flagstaffs from which floated the national colors. Other streets in the city also were dressed in holiday attire, all the enterprise of patriotic private citizens.

CENTENNIAL MEDAL

A handsome medal was struck to commemorate the event. It was designed by Mr. GEORGE W. CASILEAR, and struck on silver, bronze, and white metal gilded. On one side is shown the east front of the Capitol of the United States as of the date September 18, 1893. Above is the legend "Centennial ceremonies" and below "At the United States Capital," the whole circled with forty-four stars, with the date "Sept. 18, 1893." On the obverse is a facsimile of the scene on the bronze door of the Senate wing of the Capitol, with a medallion head of WASHINGTON, above which are fifteen stars, the whole circled with the legend "Laying the corner stone of the Capitol, September 18, 1793." The medal is suspended by a red, white, and blue silk ribbon, upon a white silk ribbon, from a bar formed in the fashion of the fasces, with bands upon which are the legend "E pluribus unum." A facsimile of the medal will be found facing this page.

SOUVENIR INVITATIONS

Handsome invitations, two thousand in number, containing the programme of the exercises at the Capitol, were prepared under the direction of the Invitation Committee and issued to distinguished guests. Upon the first exterior page was a beautiful engraving, sketching the Capitol as it appeared in 1893 from the northeast, and the Capitol as of 1851, viewed from the west, the two joined by an exact reproduction of CRAWFORD'S bronze

representation of the laying of the corner stone in 1793. The last exterior page was embellished with an engraving of the marble clock over the north door of the old Hall of the House of Representatives, now known as Statuary Hall.

THE TABLET

After defraying all the expenses incurred on account of the celebration, the Citizens' Committee had a surplus on hand, part of which was appropriated for the preparation of the account of the proceedings and of procuring suitable photographs of the Capitol to illustrate the book ordered by the Congress to be published. In addition, the sum of $900 was appropriated to secure designs for and the casting of a tablet of bronze to mark the corner stone of the original Capitol building. The contract for this tablet was given to MAURICE POWERS, of New York, whose design was accepted by the committee, and, under the joint resolution of Congress, approved April 8, 1894 (see pages 108-110), the same has been placed upon the southeast wall of the north wing of the original building, just above the corner stone laid by GEORGE WASHINGTON September 18, 1793. A facsimile of the bronze tablet will be seen facing page 109.

The estimated cost of the tablet was $1,100, but the contractor abated the sum to $900.

COST OF THE CELEBRATION

The entire expense of the celebration, as has been before said, was defrayed by the Citizens' Committee. The total amount contributed by voluntary subscriptions was $5,300.50; receipts from the concert at Convention Hall given by the Centennial Chorus, $233.30; receipts from sale of old material, $34; sales of Centennial medals to members of committee, $457.75; a total of $6,025.55. The amount of disbursements for the celebration up to the final meeting of the Citizens' Committee, April 19, 1894, was $4,797.60; leaving a cash balance on hand at that date of $1,227.95. Of this amount the sum of $100 was appropriated to

reimburse the Veteran Firemen's Association for expenditures
made by them in entertaining guests from abroad; $150 for pre-
paring the book and photographs, as before stated; $900 for the
tablet, and the remainder for the expenses incident to the preparation of the memorial.

The Parade

The Parade

On the morning of September 18, 1893, at 9 o'clock, the celebration began with the concert by the Centennial Chimes, the programme of which has been heretofore given, closing a little after 10 o'clock. At 1 o'clock the afternoon programme for the bells began, lasting until nearly 2 o'clock, and being completed just as President CLEVELAND descended from his carriage to take his seat upon the grand stand.

Long before the hour announced for the parade the route was lined with spectators, and it is estimated that over one hundred and fifty thousand people saw the pageant pass in review, while in the Capitol Grounds and the adjacent streets there were assembled not less than one hundred thousand citizens.

The following order of Chief Marshal ORDWAY for the formation and movement of the procession was adhered to with few departures:

1. The chief marshal and staff will assemble on Executive avenue, west of the Treasury Department, at 12.30 o'clock p. m.

H. Mis. 211——3

2. The cavalry escort of the President of the United States will assemble at 12.45 o'clock p. m. in inverted order, facing south, on the north side of Pennsylvania avenue, left resting on Jackson place. Carriages of orator, Chairman of General Committee, and guests on south side of Pennsylvania avenue, between west gate of the Executive Mansion and the War Department.

3. The first division will assemble at 12 o'clock m., as follows: Alexandria Washington Lodge of Masons, and the Independent Order of Odd Fellows on their left, on Jackson place, right resting on Pennsylvania avenue; the remainder of the division, in the order hereinafter named, on the south side of Pennsylvania avenue, with the Association of Oldest Inhabitants on the right, resting opposite east corner of the War Department.

4. The second division will assemble at 12.15 o'clock p. m. on Seventeenth street, south of Pennsylvania avenue, in the order hereinafter stated, right resting on Pennsylvania avenue, with its left resting on New York avenue.

5. The third division will assemble at 12.30 o'clock p. m., as follows: The United States artillery and the United States Marine Corps on the north roadway of the White Lot, right resting on Seventeenth street; the District National Guard on the west and south roadway of the White Lot, right resting at junction of north roadway.

6. The fourth division will assemble at 12.45 o'clock p. m., as follows: Veteran and visiting firemen on Lafayette place, right resting on Pennsylvania avenue; the District Fire Department on Fifteenth street, north of Pennsylvania avenue, right resting on New York avenue.

7. All organizations will assemble and stand in column, and will move in the order above stated. In proceeding to the place of assembly no organization except military will be permitted to march on Pennsylvania avenue between First and Fifteenth streets after 12 o'clock noon.

8. The procession will move precisely at 1 o'clock p. m. Any organization not in column and ready to move at that time will be excluded.

9. Carriages will march in column of twos. Civic organizations will march in column of fours, with a distance of forty-four inches between each set of fours and a distance of ten yards between organizations. Military organizations will march in column of companies or platoons, according to their strength. The distance between divisions will be forty yards.

10. The line of march will be as follows: Fifteenth street; Pennsylvania avenue to First street; through Capitol Grounds, north of the Capitol, to B street north; B street north to First street east; First street east to B street south; B street south to New Jersey avenue. Organizations will be dismissed from the procession on reaching the corner of B street south and New Jersey avenue. Music will not be permitted to play on Capitol Hill after 2 o'clock p. m.

11. The organization and order of the procession will be as follows:

Chief Marshal and staff.
Squadron of United States cavalry.
President of the United States.
Orator of the day.
Governors of States.
Chairman of General Committee; distinguished guests.
Troop A, District National Guard.

FIRST DIVISION

RALPH L. GALT, Marshal.

Alexandria Washington Lodge of Masons.
Independent Order of Odd Fellows.
Association of the Oldest Inhabitants.

Order of Elks.
Knights of Pythias.
Order of United American Mechanics.
Order of Red Men.
Knights of St. Peter.
Independent Order of Rechabites of North America.
Journeymen Stonecutters' Association of the District of Columbia.
Capital City Guards.
Butler Infantry Corps.

SECOND DIVISION

WILLIAM P. YOUNG, Marshal.

National Rifles.
Society of the Cincinnati.
Sons of the American Revolution.
Sons of the Revolution.
Society of Colonial Wars.
Aztec Club of 1847.
Veterans of the Mexican War.
Old Guard
Grand Army of the Republic.
Sons of Veterans.

THIRD DIVISION

General H. G. GIBSON, U. S. A., Marshal.

Battalion of Fourth United States Artillery.
Light Battery C, Third United States Artillery.
Battalion of United States Marine Corps.
National Guard of the District of Columbia.
Company F, Third Regiment Virginia Volunteers.

FOURTH DIVISION

Mr. JAMES H. RICHARDS, Marshal.

Veteran Firemen of the District of Columbia.
Veteran Firemen of Brooklyn, N. Y.
Hydraulion Fire Company of Alexandria, Va.
Relief Hook and Ladder Company of Alexandria, Va.
Fire Department of Frederick, Md.
Fire Department of the District of Columbia.

By order of Chief Marshal ALBERT ORDWAY:

ELLIS SPEAR, *Chief of Staff.*

A T 12.45 o'clock Mr. LAWRENCE GARDNER, Chairman of the General Committee, and Mr. BERIAH WILKINS, Chairman of the Reception Committee, reported to President CLEVELAND that the parade was formed, and, escorted by Mr. WILKINS, the President entered the carriage assigned to him and rapidly drove to his place in the column.

General ALBERT ORDWAY, the Grand Marshal, then rode to the front of the column, and the parade marched down Fifteenth street to Pennsylvania avenue, thence to the Capitol, over the designated route, in the following order:

General ALBERT ORDWAY, Chief Marshal ; General ELLIS SPEAR, Chief of Staff, and the aids heretofore named.

United States cavalry, Colonel GUY V. HENRY commanding :

    Troop A, First United States Cavalry, Captain BOMAS.

    Troop H, Eighth United States Cavalry, Lieutenant STEELE.

    Troop F, Seventh United States Cavalry, Captain BELL.

    Troop K, Ninth United States Cavalry, Captain HUGHES.

Colonel H. C. CORBIN, U. S. A., and Captain GEORGE C. SCHRIVER, U. S. A., special aids.

The President of the United States, Chairman of Ceremonies, in carriage with Mr. BERIAH WILKINS, Chairman of Committee on Reception.

WILLIAM WIRT HENRY, orator of the day, escorted by Mr. LAWRENCE GARDNER, Chairman of the General Committee.

The Secretary of State, escorted by Dr. J. M. TONER and Mr. WILLIAM B. WEBB.

The Secretary of the Treasury, escorted by Mr. J. W. BABSON and Mr. MATTHEW G. EMERY.

The Attorney-General, escorted by General S. S. HENKLE and Mr. HENRY WISE GARNETT.

The Postmaster-General, escorted by Mr. CHARLES C. GLOVER and Dr. WILLIAM TINDALL.

The Secretary of Agriculture, escorted by Mr. SIMON WOLF and Mr. H. W. SOHON.

The Right Reverend WILLIAM PARET, Bishop of Maryland, escorted by Mr. A. R. SPOFFORD and Mr. E. B. HAY.

The Justices of the United States Supreme Court, escorted by Messrs. ENOCH TOTTEN, CHAPIN BROWN, WILLIAM F. MATTINGLY, and A. S. WORTHINGTON.

The Joint Committee of Congress, escorted by Messrs. B. H. WARNER, ISADORE

36

SAKS, MARSHALL W. WINES, HARRISON DINGMAN, and L. C. WILLIAMSON.
The Commissioners of the District of Columbia, escorted by Mr. M. I. WELLER.
The Court of Appeals, District of Columbia.
The Supreme Court of the District of Columbia.
The Governor of Maryland and the Governor of Rhode Island, escorted by Mr.
F. A. LEHMAN and Mr. A. F. SPERRY.
Troop A, District National Guard.

FIRST DIVISION.

RALPH L. GALT, Marshal, and aids.

Association of the Oldest Inhabitants, E. R. McKEAN, Marshal.
Independent Order of Odd Fellows, Dr. T. J. JONES, Marshal:
  Grand Encampment.
  Subordinate Encampment.
  Grand Lodge.
  Subordinate Lodge.
  Grand Canton, No. 1, of Baltimore, Md.
  Monumental Canton, of Baltimore, Md.
  Zimmerman Canton, of Baltimore, Md.
Uniform Rank Knights of Pythias, Colonel H. C. COGGIN commanding.
Benevolent Order of Elks, SAMUEL KING, Marshal:
  Washington Lodge, No. 15.
  Baltimore Lodge, No. 7.
Order of Red Men, JOHN C. DENNING, Marshal.
United Order of American Mechanics, JOHN D. SCHOFIELD, Marshal.
Junior Order of American Mechanics, W. W. BOSWELL, Marshal.
Sons of Jonadab.
Independent Order of Rechabites:
  Senior Order, J. ADAMS, Marshal.
  Junior Order, JOHN R. MAHONY, Marshal.
Capital City Guards.
Butler Cadets.

SECOND DIVISION

WILLIAM P. YOUNG, Marshal, and aids.

National Rifles, Captain JAMES F. OYSTER commanding.
Officers of the General Society and officers of the State and District societies of the Sons of the American Revolution, in carriages. They were: General HORACE PORTER, of New York, President-General; General J. C. BRECKINRIDGE, U. S. A., Vice-President-General; Hon. FRANKLIN MURPHY, of New York, Secretary-General; Mr. C. W. HASKINS, of New York, Treasurer-General; Mr. A. HOWARD CLARKE, of Washington, D. C., Registrar-General; Rev. Dr. RANDOLPH McKIM, of Washington, D. C., chaplain; Mr. E. M. GALLAUDET, of Washington, D. C., President of the District of Columbia society; Judge JOHN GOODE, of Virginia; Hon. HENRY M. SHEPARD, President of the society in Illinois; Hon. E. C. CABELL, President of the society in Missouri; Mr. ALEXANDER HAMILTON, of New York.
Society of the Cincinnati, in carriages, by the following committee: Hon. ASA BIRD GARDINER, LL.D., Secretary-General; Hon. CLIFFORD STANLEY, of New Jersey; Colonel GEORGE B. SANFORD, U. S. A.; Mr. JOHN CROPPER, New York; Hon. WILLIAM WAYNE, Pennsylvania; Hon. WILLIAM B. WEBB, LL.D., Maryland;

General GEORGE DOHERTY JOHNSON, South Carolina; Hon. WILLIAM D. HAR-
DEN, Georgia; Mr. OSCEOLA C. GREEN, Maryland; Mr. HENRY RANDALL WEBB,
Maryland, and Mr. WILLIAM MacPHERSON HORNOR, Pennsylvania.
  Sons of the Revolution.
  Society of Colonial Wars.
  Sons of the American Revolution, Hon. JOHN W. DOUGLASS, Marshal.
  The Old Guard.
  The Grand Army of the Republic, Junior Vice-Commander B. T. JANNEY com-
manding.
    John A. Rawlins Post, No. 1, S. W. TULEY commanding.
    Kit Carson Post, No. 2, A. HART commanding.
    George G. Meade Post, No. 5, E. C. GRUMLEY commanding.
    Lincoln Post, No. 3, DANIEL WILLIAMS commanding.
    John F. Reynolds Post, No. 6, W. N. THOMAS commanding.
    J. A. Garfield Post, No. 7, T. R. SENIOR commanding.
    O. P. Morton Post, No. 7, WALTER MIDDLETON commanding.
    Farragut Post, No. 10, A. B. HURLBURT commanding.
    Charles P. Stone Post, No. 11, W. H. HOOVER commanding.
    George W. Morris Post, No. 19, SAMUEL McGONNIGLE commanding.
    Sheridan Post, No. 14, H. E. BURTON commanding.
    George H. Somers Post, No. 15, B. FULLER commanding.
    George H. Thomas Post, No. 13, A. B. FRISBIE commanding.
    Henry Wilson Post, No. 17, W. S. DEERE commanding.
  Sons of Veterans, CHARLES CONRAD commanding:
    John A. Logan Post, No. 2.

THIRD DIVISION

General H. G. GIBSON, U. S. A., Marshal, and aids.

  Fourth Artillery Band.
  Companies M, I, and A, Fourth United States Artillery, Captain FUGER, U. S. A.,
commanding battalion.
  Marine Band, Professor FANCIULLI, Director.
  Marine Corps, four companies, Lieutenant H. K. WHITE commanding battalion.
  District National Guard, Colonel CECIL CLAY commanding, and staff:
    Schroeder's National Guard Band.
    Engineer Corps, Lieutenant F. S. AVERILL.
    First Regiment of Infantry, Colonel WILLIAM G. MOORE commanding and
      staff.
    First Battalion (Light Infantry), Major BURTON R. ROSS, commanding:
      Company A, Captain C. M. LOEFFLER.
      Company B, Captain C. M. SHREVE.
      Company C, Captain C. H. OURAND.
      Company D, Captain JOHN S. MILLER.
    Second Battalion, Major R. A. O'BRIEN commanding:
      Company A, Corcoran Cadets, Captain E. C. EDWARDS.
      Company B, Morton Cadets, Captain L. H. REICHELFELDER.
      Company C, National Fencibles, Captain C. S. DOMER.
      Company D, High School Cadets, Captain R. H. YOUNG.
      War Department Guards, Captain F. T. WILSON.
    Second Regiment of Infantry, Lieutenant-Colonel M. EMMETT URELL com-
      manding and staff.

Fourth Battalion, Major E. R. CAMPBELL, commanding:
  Company A, Emmet Guards, Captain HARRY WALSH.
  Company B, Columbian Guards, Lieutenant J. F. KELLY.
  Company D, Ordway Rifles, Captain J. M. WILLIAMS.
Fifth Battalion, Major OTTO L. SCESS commanding:
  Company A, Captain W. J. SIMMONS.
  Company B, Captain FABIAN COLUMBUS.
  Company C, Lieutenant SWIGART.
  Company C, Lieutenant G. W. ENGLAND.
Sixth Battalion, Captain J. A. SALMON commanding:
  Company A, Captain JOHN W. PARSONS.
  Company B, Captain J. S. TOMLINSON.
  Company C, Captain E. D. SMOOT.
  Company D, Lieutenant H. L. B. ACKERSON.
Battery A, Captain H. G. FORSBERG commanding.
Ambulance Corps, Lieutenants J. A. WATSON and D. S. VERDI.
Bicycle Corps, Captain C. B. STORY.

FOURTH DIVISION

Colonel JAMES H. RICHARDS, Marshal.

Laurel Military Band.
Washington Veteran Firemen, with engine and hose wagon, JOHN THOMPSON, Foreman.
Freeport Cornet Band.
Brooklyn Veteran Firemen, J. H. BERGER, Marshal.
Alexandria Hydraulion and Relief Company, with engine, hose carriage, and fuel wagon, Sergeant CROUSE commanding.
Alexandria Hook and Ladder Company, R. M. LATHAM, Foreman.
District Fire Department, Chief PARRIS and Assistant Chief BELT.
  Engines and hose carriages:
    No. 1.
    No. 2.
    No. 4.
    No. 6.
    No. 7.
    Truck A.
    Fuel and supply wagons.
Battalion Mounted Police.

At the Capitol

49

At the Capitol

Long before the appointed hour for the commencement of the exercises at the Capitol, the invited guests, who were received at the east door of the Rotunda by General DUNCAN S. WALKER, Chairman of the Committee on Invitations, and his assistants, began to arrive and were shown to their seats upon the grand  stand. Besides the President and the orators of the day, the Cabinet, the Justices of the Supreme Court, Chiefs of Bureaus in the Executive Departments, distinguished officers of the Army and Navy, members

of the Diplomatic Corps, and other eminent persons, numbering two thousand, had been invited, and the stand was filled to its utmost capacity.

At a few minutes before 2 o'clock, the Senate, in a body, preceded by its President, Sergeant-at-Arms, Secretary, and Doorkeeper, passed through the Rotunda and entered the stand to the north, provided for the Congress.

45

Almost immediately afterwards the House of Representatives, preceded by its Speaker, Clerk, Sergeant-at-Arms, and Doorkeeper, passed through the east door of the Rotunda and took the seats assigned them on the north stand.

In a few minutes the Joint Committee of Congress appeared upon the grand stand, and as the head of the column arrived, President CLEVELAND, who was to act as the Chairman of Ceremonies, the Right Reverend the Bishop of Maryland, and the orators of the day, escorted by members of the Citizens' Committee, alighted from their carriages and took seats in the front of the central stand, welcomed by a great shout arising from one hundred thousand throats.

Already Professor CLOWARD had occupied the south stand with his fifteen hundred choristers. The Marine Band, Professor FANCIULLI, had been unavoidably detained for a few moments, due to the fact that they marched in the parade at the head of the Marine Corps. In the meantime the chimes at the Congressional Library building, directly in front of the grounds, rang out a merry peal, while the crowd cheered again and again.

THE INVOCATION

The Chairman of the Citizens' Committee arose, and by his gestures commanded silence. The assemblage obeyed, and at 2.07 p. m. the Right Reverend WILLIAM PARET, Bishop of Maryland, vested in his episcopal robes, advanced to the front of the platform and made the invocation, as follows:

Direct us, O Lord, in all our doings with Thy most gracious favor, and further us with Thy continual help; that in all our works begun, continued, and ended in Thee we may glorify Thy holy Name, and finally, by Thy mercy, obtain everlasting life, through Jesus Christ our Lord. *Amen.*

Our Father who art in heaven, hallowed be Thy Name. Thy kingdom come. Thy will be done on earth, as it is in heaven. Give us this day our daily bread. And forgive us our trespasses, as we forgive those who trespass against us. And lead us not into temptation, but deliver us from evil: For Thine is the kingdom and the power and the glory, for ever and ever. *Amen.*

Almighty God, whose kingdom is everlasting and power infinite, have mercy upon this whole land; and so rule the hearts of Thy servants, the President of the United States and all others in authority, that they, knowing whose ministers they are, may above all things seek Thine honor and glory; and that we and all the people, duly considering whose authority they bear, may faithfully and obediently honor them, in Thee, and for Thee, according to Thy blessed Word and ordinance; through Jesus Christ our Lord, who, with Thee and the Holy Ghost, liveth and reigneth, ever one God, world without end. *Amen.*

Most gracious God, we humbly beseech Thee, as for the people of these United States in general, so especially for their Senate and Representatives in Congress assembled, that Thou wouldst be pleased to direct and prosper all their consultations, to the advancement of Thy glory, the good of Thy church, the safety, honor, and welfare of Thy people; that all things may be so ordered and settled by their endeavors, upon the best and surest foundations, that peace and happiness, truth and justice, religion and piety, may be established among us for all generations. These and all other necessaries, for them, for us, and Thy whole church, we humbly beg in the name and mediation of Jesus Christ our most blessed Lord and Savior. *Amen.*

Almighty Father, from whose goodness it comes that this house has been and is the center of a powerful and happy nation, most heartily we thank Thee for all Thy loving providences to these United States: And this day especially, that Thou hast so guided the wisdom and overruled all the errors and prejudices of our great national counsels and decisions for these one hundred years. Accept our thankfulness, we beseech Thee, for the sake of Jesus Christ our Lord. *Amen.*

O God, who holdest in Thy hand, but hidest from us, all the issues of the future years, we beseech Thee to continue over these United States Thy watchful and restraining love. Guide our statesmen and our magistrates and judges to all that is needful for us, in peace and truth and righteousness. Restrain them, we beseech Thee, from all injustice, oppression, or wrong. May the truth and justice of God and the welfare of the people rule all their actions.

And if it be Thy will that at the end of another century these walls shall still be standing, grant that they may stand with our nation's truth and honor steadfast and untarnished.

All which we ask for the sake of Jesus Christ our Lord. *Amen.*

The Grand Centennial Chorus, accompanied by the United States Marine Band, then sang the ''Te Deum.''

CHAIRMAN GARDNER'S INTRODUCTION

Mr. LAWRENCE GARDNER, Chairman of the Citizens' Committee, then spoke as follows:

One hundred years ago GEORGE WASHINGTON, the first President of the United States, standing on this hillside, then almost a wilderness, laid the corner stone of the permanent home of Congress, in whose majestic shadow we are now assembled. Our written Constitution, the beacon light of every freeman, was then but an experiment, of which the creation of a national capital, under the exclusive control of the legislature, was the most novel feature. Washington City was

a name; the United States a federation of fifteen States, sparsely populated, bounded on the west by the Mississippi, and with no port upon the great Gulf.

How conditions have changed since WASHINGTON last stood near this hallowed spot! To-day the population of the country exceeds that of any English-speaking people; its area has been enlarged from 927,000 to 3,604,000 square miles; its boundaries are washed by the two great oceans. To-day we more than realize the hope here expressed by WASHINGTON, before an assemblage small in numbers, but strong in that faith that overcometh all human obstacles.

As the country grew, so grew its Capitol, year by year, stone upon stone, until, on this its hundredth anniversary, it shows forth the most magnificent structure of any age, crowning the most beautiful city of the world.

Gentlemen of the Senate and House of Representatives, as we now commemorate the laying of the corner stone of your legislative home, it is meet to give thanks for the preeminent part taken by Congress in the wonderful development of the system of government to which the United States owes its sure and rapid advancement.

CEREMONIES AT CAPITOL SEPTEMBER 18, 1893.

To Congress the country is indebted for the fundamental acts which rounded out the frame of the organic law and gave life and vigor to all its parts. A study of the history of legislative bodies in all lands and times will disclose none the superior of the American Congress, whether in intelligence, patriotism, or in purity of purpose.

Ladies and gentlemen, I will not detain you longer. Under the direction of the Joint Committee of Congress I have now the pleasure of introducing to you as Chairman of Ceremonies the worthy successor of WASHINGTON, the President of the United States, GROVER CLEVELAND.

PRESIDENT CLEVELAND'S ADDRESS

As President CLEVELAND, the Chairman of Ceremonies, arose and removed his hat, taking his stand near the familiar spot occupied by him twice before on the occasion of his first and second inaugural addresses, the crowd in front broke into a cheer which was taken up by the vast throngs beyond.

The President said:

While I accept with much satisfaction the part assigned to me on this occasion, I can not escape the sober reflections which these ceremonies suggest. Those who suppose that we are simply engaged in commemorating the beginning of a magnificent structure devoted to important public uses have overlooked the most useful and improving lesson of the hour. We do indeed celebrate the laying of a corner stone from which has sprung the splendid edifice whose grand proportions arouse the pride of every American citizen, but our celebration is chiefly valuable and significant because this edifice was designed and planned by great and good men as a place where the principles of a free representative government should be developed in patriotic legislation for the benefit of free people. If representatives who here assemble to make laws for their fellow-countrymen forget the duty of broad and disinterested patriotism and legislate in prejudice and passion or in behalf of sectional and selfish interests, the time when the corner stone of our Capitol was laid and the circumstances surrounding it will not be worth commemorating.

The sentiment and the traditions connected with this structure and its uses belong to all the people of the land. They are most valuable as reminders of patriotism in the discharge of public duty and steadfastness in many a struggle for the public good. They also furnish a standard by which our people may measure the conduct of those chosen to serve them. The inexorable application of this standard will always supply proof that our countrymen realize the value of the free institutions which were designed and built by those who laid the corner stone of their Capitol, and that they appreciate the necessity of constant and jealous watchfulness as a condition indispensable to the preservation of these institutions in their purity and integrity.

I believe our fellow-citizens have no greater nor better cause for rejoicing on this centennial than is found in the assurance that their public servants who assemble in these halls will watch and guard the sentiment and traditions that gather around this celebration, and that in the days to come those who shall again commemorate the laying of the corner stone of their nation's Capitol will find in the recital of our performance of public duty no less reason for enthusiasm and congratulation than we find in recalling the wisdom and virtue of those who have preceded us.

When the Chairman of Ceremonies concluded his address the cheering was prolonged, and only ceased when the Marine Band rendered selections from "Lakmé."

WILLIAM WIRT HENRY'S ORATION

The Chairman of Ceremonies, President CLEVELAND, then arose and briefly introduced the orator of the day, Mr. WILLIAM WIRT HENRY, of Virginia, as the able and eloquent descendant of PATRICK HENRY.

Mr. HENRY then spoke as follows:

FELLOW-CITIZENS OF THE UNITED STATES: The exercises of to-day are a fitting close of the series of centennial celebrations of the most important events in our Revolutionary history. Celebrations which have presented vividly to the present generation the courage of our ancestors in winning our liberties, and their wisdom in forming a system of government which has proved a safeguard of the invaluable possession. From the skirmish at Lexington on April 19, 1775, when the *immedicabile vulnus* was inflicted which finally severed the ligament binding the Colonies to the mother country, to April 30, 1789, when WASHINGTON was inaugurated as the first President under the Federal Constitution, the most important events have been made to pass in panorama before our eyes. The attention of the world has been more closely attracted by us, and American history has assumed its proper position in the forefront, where it is destined to remain as the great teacher of advanced civilization. And now it becomes us to celebrate the hundredth anniversary of the laying of the corner stone of this magnificent Capitol, the permanent home of the Government of this great nation, and thus to complete the roll call of the events which established us among the nations of the earth.

In looking back upon these events how insignificant they appeared at the time to the outside world! Our battles were but skirmishes as compared with the engagements of the vast armies which had reddened the soil of Europe and Asia in their conflicts. Our Declaration of Independence was but *brutum fulmen* unless sustained by force of arms, which was believed to be beyond our power. Our first union was held by a rope of sand, and even our Federal Constitution, dependent as it was upon popular will, was an experiment with a divided people — divided as to the wisdom of the plan, and divided as to the construction of the instrument. It was confidently predicted by the enemies of our free institutions that our experiment would prove a miserable failure, and that but a short distance would intervene between its cradle and its grave.

But how different the scene of to-day! What grand results have followed from our despised beginnings! For more than a century we have demonstrated, as no other people have ever done before, our capacity for self-government. Our Federal system has been tested in peace and in war, and by violent forces from without and within, yet every fiber has stood the strain, and its perfect adaptation to our needs under all circumstances has been demonstrated. Yea, more; already the hope of our fathers as to the effect of our free institutions upon the human race has been wonderfully realized. That hope  was expressed by JAMES WILSON in the Pennsylvania Convention which adopted the Constitution when he said:

By adopting this system we shall probably lay a foundation for erecting temples of liberty in every part of the earth. It has been thought by many that on the success of the struggle America has made for freedom will depend the exertions of the brave and enlightened of other nations. The advantages resulting from this system will not be confined to the United States, but will draw from Europe many worthy characters who pant for the enjoyment of freedom. It will induce princes, in order to preserve their subjects, to restore to them a portion of that liberty of which they have for many ages been deprived. It will be subservient to the great designs of Providence with regard to this globe—the multiplication of mankind, their improvement in knowledge and their advancement in happiness.

It takes but a cursory view of the present condition of the people of Christendom to recognize the liberalizing effect of our Government upon their civil institutions. It has been well said by a late writer that "at the close of the American Revolution there was in the Old World only one free nation and no democracy. In Europe there

now remain but two strong monarchies—those of Russia and Prussia—
while America, scarcely excepting Brazil and Canada, is entirely (at
least in name) republican." Since he wrote Brazil has dethroned her
king and adopted a republican form of government, and there is a
strong movement in Canada toward union with the United States.
But while other nations have followed more or less closely in our
footsteps, striving to enjoy our freedom, how wonderful has been
our progress in all that makes a nation great! When we consider the
enlarged extent of our territory, the increase of our population, our
progress in the arts and sciences, in commerce, in wealth, and in
knowledge, we are forced to exclaim, "God has blessed us, and has
made His face to shine upon us!"

With the history of this progress this Capitol has been intimately
connected. Here the Chief Executives of the nation have taken the
oath of office and made their communications to Congress. Here the
wise men of the nation have discussed and formulated the great measures of internal and external policy which have placed us in the front
rank of the nations of the earth. Here treaties with foreign nations
have been confirmed. Here territory has been annexed, out of which
new States have been constituted, until, instead of fifteen States east
of the Mississippi, we have stretched across the continent, and now
number forty-four States, whose eastern and western shores are washed
by the great oceans on whose bosoms our commerce is borne to every
quarter of the globe. Here our Supreme Court has been seated, the
most important tribunal which has ever existed, and great jurists have
decided grave questions between the States, and have construed our
system of government, defining and limiting the powers of each
department and confining it to its appropriate sphere. Here representatives of foreign nations have watched the working of our free
institutions, and have realized the capacity of man for self-government.

When we remember the great men who have shed luster on this
Capitol during the past century, as Presidents, legislators, and jurists,
we can justly claim an eminence for our Republic which has not been
excelled, if ever equaled, by any other nation of this or any other age.

Nor has this city, located by WASHINGTON and bearing his honored
name, failed to realize the expectation of its founder that it would
become the fitting capital of a great nation. It is now justly claimed
to be one of the most beautiful and attractive of the capitals of the
world. Within the century, the scoffing lines of the poet have become
a splendid reality. Could he, who in 1804 wrote of the scattered
village—

> This embryo capital, where fancy sees
> Squares in morasses, obelisks in trees;
> Which second-sighted seers even now adorn
> With shrines unbuilt, and heroes yet unborn—

look upon this city to-day, with its quarter of a million of inhabitants, its beautiful streets and squares bordered with costly residences, its splendid monuments and its magnificent public buildings, he would realize that the "fancies of the second-sighted seers" of his day have been more than fulfilled as real prophecies.

As I stand here on this commemoration day, two periods in the history of this building rise prominent to my view: the first, at the beginning of the century which ends to-day. I behold a country not yet recovered from the exhaustion of the war which established its independence; with a new system of government not sufficiently tried to overcome the friction of its machinery, nor to insure its stability and its capacity to check the spirit of anarchy which had been so strongly manifested in the nation, and had so seriously threatened the dissolution of the Union; with a  revenue inadequate to meet its liabilities; without sufficient strength to force England to comply with the terms of her treaty and surrender the military posts on the Great Lakes, and as a consequence suffering the cruel effects of an Indian war believed to have been instigated by the British commanders; with Spain plotting to get a foothold in the Mississippi Valley, by refusing to the United States the free navigation of that river, whose mouth she held, and offering it to the inhabitants of the valley as the price of their leaving the Union and casting their lot with her; with open opposition to the excise law of Congress, assuming the form of an insurrection in west Pennsylvania; but above all with the almost maddening effect upon the people of the French Revolution, followed by war between France and England, which was threatening to engulf the newly launched American ship of state in the maelstrom of European wars. I see the calm figure of WASHINGTON holding firmly the helm of state as he steers it amidst the storm, and with that unfaltering faith in the future of his country which had nerved him to be her deliverer in her darkest hours of trial, coming to this spot to lay the corner stone of the Capitol of the nation he had created, and which he firmly believed would be not only the freest but one of the greatest which the world had ever known. Behold that majestic form, erect, though burdened with the cares of state, and carrying the weight of over three-score years, attired with the simple emblems of masonry, descending into the trench and laying his hand on the corner stone on which was to be erected the permanent Capitol of the United States of America; a foreshadowing of the time, near at hand, when, divested of all earthly cares, he was to descend into the tomb, laying his hand of faith on the corner stone not laid with hands, on which was to be reared his eternal mansion in the heavens.

But the scene changes. More than a half century has passed, during which we have engaged in two wars, one with England, in which we contested her sovereignty of the seas, and the other with Mexico, resulting in a large accession to our western territory, already greatly enlarged by treaty. In the meanwhile portentous questions have arisen between the Northern and Southern States, threatening a dissolution of the Union. African slavery, that baneful legacy of our mother country, had been cast out of the Northern States, where it had ceased to be profitable, and had become more deeply rooted in the Southern States, whose climate and agricultural system were better suited to its existence. A bitter contest had consequently sprung up between the sections over the balance of power in the administration of the Federal Government. This was made the more alarming by the radical difference in the constructions given to the Federal system. By the one party it was held to be a government of a nation, and that by the adoption of the Federal Constitution each State had merged a part of its sovereignty into that of the whole, which could not be recalled except by successful revolution. By the other party the Federal Constitution was held to be a compact between sovereign States, each of which had the right to pass upon the legality of Federal acts, to nullify their operation, if deemed an infraction of the compact, and, as a last resort, to secede from the Union. With such a view of the Federal system it is no wonder that many threats of secession had been made by parties North and South dissatisfied with Federal laws. California had been acquired from Mexico, and, rich in gold, it had been soon filled with a population sufficient to form a State. A convention of its people framed a constitution which excluded slavery from its borders, and with this instrument in hand they knocked at the door of Congress for admission during the session of 1849–50. To admit her was to destroy the equilibrium between the free and slave States, and therefore a fierce struggle at once arose which threatened the permanency of the Union. Happily two of the greatest statesmen and purest patriots our country has ever produced were in the councils of the nation, HENRY CLAY, of Kentucky, and DANIEL WEBSTER, of Massachusetts. By their combined efforts the compromise measures of 1850 were enacted, which it was fondly hoped would settle the sectional strife.

It was at this period that the growth of the nation demanded an enlargement of its Capitol. The Fourth of July, 1851, was fixed for the laying of the corner stone of the addition, and the great expounder and defender of the Constitution, the foremost of living statesmen, the matchless orator, DANIEL WEBSTER, was selected to make the address. Those who remember him as he lived and moved among men easily recall the massive head, the deep-toned voice, the grand periods, the profound thought, which held his auditors spellbound whenever he spoke. On this occasion we see him but lately transferred from the Senate to the foremost seat in the Cabinet, the conspicuous mark for the arrows of sectionalism; yet, firmly fixed in the position he had assumed in his celebrated speech on the compromise measures, delivered in the Senate the 7th of March, 1850, in which, filled with the patriotism which animated the first Continental Congress, he had uttered the memorable words, "I wish to speak to-day not as a Massachusetts man, nor as a Northern man, but as an American." Fit successor of the Father of his Country in the ceremonies of the day, we see his faith in the future of the Union emerging from the cloud which had overshadowed the political horizon, and while he recounts the unprecedented happiness and the wonderful progress of the country under the Federal Government, he appeals to the dissatisfied to exorcise the spirit of disunion, and to cling to the Government framed by their forefathers as the sheet anchor  of their liberties, the ark of their safety, the assurance, doubly sure, of their ever-increasing greatness.

Sectional strife was not, indeed, quelled by the compromise of 1850, but fuel was continually added to the flame, till secession, so long threatened, was at last attempted by the Southern States. In the terrible civil war that followed slavery and secession went down together, clasped in the embrace of eternal death, and the Union survived, more firmly knit by the effort to disrupt it, and blessing a nation of freemen. It remains for us now to cast out the spirit of sectionalism, that bitter fountain of our woes, and henceforth to unite to realize the sentiment of the poet—

> One flag, one land, one heart, one hand,
> One nation evermore!

In the address of Mr. WEBSTER on the Fourth of July, 1851, he gave a comparative table of statistics showing the growth of the nation between 1793 and 1851. Extending a few of the items of this table to the present date, and using reports for 1892 in doing so, we can realize our growth within the last forty-two years.

	1793.	1851.	1892.
Number of States	15	31	44
Population of United States	3,984,328	23,267,448	*65,000,000
Amount of receipts into Treasury	$5,720,624	$52,312,952	$425,868,260
Amount of exports	$26,109,000	$217,517,130	$1,075,818,180
Amount of imports	$31,000,000	$215,725,995	$827,087,003
Area of United States in square miles	804,164	3,314,365	3,602,990
Number of miles of railroad..........................	...	10,287	218,528
Number of miles of electric telegraph...............		15,000	250,000
Number of miles of telephone		....	239,000
Number of universities and colleges	19	121	420

* Estimated.

The Christian churches have more than kept pace with the increase of population, and they have at least 16,000,000 members. Nor are we behind any other nation in our charitable institutions and common schools.

As our wonderful progress as a nation is mainly due to our free institutions, it seems appropriate to this occasion that we review briefly their origin and growth. Let us approach the task reverently, for in listening to the voice of history we will recognize the voice of God, and in studying the past aright we must needs discover the Divinity which shapes our ends.

It is an ennobling thought that from the day that God said, " Let the waters under the heaven be gathered together unto one place, and let the dry land appear," He began to prepare this continent for the abode of our race, as the most worthy of the human family. He brought forth the mountains and filled them with all the mineral wealth needed by the most civilized of men. He placed the mountain ranges as sentinels along the shores, charging them to arrest the clouds which arise from the seas and force them to water and enrich the earth. He placed the great valleys between and caused them " to bring forth grass, the herb yielding seed, and the fruit tree yielding fruit after his kind," suited for the sustenance of a great nation. He caused deep rivers to flow from the mountains, to the north and to the south, to the east and to the west. He placed the Gulf in the south and the lakes in the north, and made them, with the rivers, convenient highways for the commerce of a great and prosperous people, and He threw over the whole the temperate zone. Having fitted this continent for the abode of a people advanced to the highest point of human

progress. He hid it from the eyes of civilized man and consigned it
to the keeping of a savage race. Ignorant of its wealth, they knew
no use of its grand forests, except to hunt in them; of its broad
rivers and lakes, except to fish in them; nor of its productive soil,
except to soak it with the blood of contending tribes. Thus this rich
continent, best fitted of all for the abode of civilized man, was guarded
and kept undisturbed for ages, till in the fullness of time God had
trained up a people worthy to enjoy it.

The wonderful training of that people is one of the grandest lessons
of history.

We have been taught that America is indebted to Great Britain for
her greatness, but in truth Great Britain is indebted to America for its
existence among the nations of the earth. The Gulf Stream, rising
in the torrid zone, after issuing from the Gulf of Mexico, takes its
course northward along the northeastern shore of North America,

by which it is deflected till it turns
across the Atlantic and reaches
the British Isles, rescuing them
from the embrace of the frigid zone,
giving them a temperate climate
suited to the development of the
highest type of manhood, and furnishing them with the moisture needed
for a rich vegetation. Through this
silent, unrecognized influence, exerted
through unnumbered years, these
isles have been made to blossom as
the rose, and enabled to sustain a
population fitted to lead the world
in the progress of civilization. It
was these favored isles which, in the
providence of God, were selected for the training of the race worthy
of the rich heritage of North America.

The Celts, their earliest inhabitants, were not of this favored race;
nor were their conquerors, the Romans. Imperial Rome regarded not
her citizens as free agents, but as blind, unquestioning parts of an
immense political machine. She based her authority upon force, not
upon the consent of the governed. Her despotic government, by
crushing all local independence, crushed all local vigor. For nearly
four hundred years the island of Britain was thus held as a province
of the Roman Empire. During this period that great power entered
upon its decline and finally tottered to its fall. In 411 A. D. the
Roman legions were withdrawn from Britain, in the vain effort to
defend Italy against the Goths. They never returned, and thus it
was ordered that the Latin race was not to possess that fair isle.

After the withdrawal of the Roman legions the Britons were set upon by the Picts of Scotland and the Scots of Ireland, and finally called to their aid the English and Saxons from their home on the peninsula which divides the waters of the Baltic from the North Sea. These came, A. D. 449, under their chiefs, HENGIST and HORSA, and having first delivered the Britons from their foes, they then overpowered them and became masters of the island. At last the race had come which was to permanently possess the island. They were of the Low German branch of the Teutonic family—a people who had withstood the arms of Rome for more than five hundred years, and were now moving from their forest homes to the attack and overthrow of that great empire.

The Germans presented a striking contrast with the Romans in their appearance, domestic life, and civil institutions. The Roman historians describe them at the beginning of the second century as follows:

A race pure, unmixed, and stamped with a distinct character. Hence a family likeness pervades the whole, though their numbers are so great; eyes stern and blue, ruddy hair, large bodies, powerful in sudden exertions, but impatient of toil and labor; fenced around with chastity, corrupted by no seductive spectacles, no convivial incitements; supposing somewhat of sanctity and prescience to be inherent in the female sex, and therefore neither despising their counsels nor disregarding their responses. Almost single among the barbarians, they content themselves with one wife. The women take one husband as one body and one life, that no thought, no desire may extend beyond him; and he may be loved not only as their husband but as their marriage. A person's own children are his heirs and successors, and no wills are made. They do not inhabit cities, or even admit of contiguous settlements. They dwell scattered and separate, as a spring, a meadow, a grove may chance to invite them. In their villages everyone surrounds his house with a vacant space. No people are more addicted to social entertainments nor more liberal in the exercise of hospitality. To refuse any person whatever admittance under their roof is accounted flagitious. Everyone, according to his ability, feasts his guest. They worship Oden as their chief divinity, and draw his character from their own, delighting to show strength in battle, and to execute vengeance on their enemies. They deem it unworthy of the grandeur of their deity to confine his worship within walls, or to represent him under a human similitude. Woods and groves are their temples, and they affix the name of Divinity to that secret power which they behold with the eye of adoration alone. Their settlements are around some tree or mound held sacred in their religious rites, and here the people assemble to transact matters of government and to decide upon war or peace. They are divided into nations, some under kings, some under chiefs. The nations are divided into cantons, each under a chief or count, who administers justice in it. The cantons are divided into districts, or hundreds, each containing a hundred vills or townships. In each hundred is a centenary, chosen by the people, before whom small cases are tried and determined, according to the customs of the settlement. Their courts of justice are held in the open air, on rising ground, beneath the shade of a large tree. They elect their kings and chiefs, having regard to birth and fitness; and their generals, having regard to valor. Their kings exercise limited authority, and their generals command less through the force of authority than example. If they are daring, adventurous, and conspicuous in action, they procure obedience from the admiration they inspire. On affairs of smaller moment, the chiefs consult; on those of greater importance, the whole community; yet with this circumstance, that what is referred to the decision of the people is first maturely discussed by the chiefs. It is customary for the several states to present, by voluntary or individual contributions, cattle or grain to their chiefs, which are accepted as honorary gifts, while they serve as necessary supplies.

In this description of this stalwart and liberty-loving people we easily recognize the rudiments of English character and English institutions, which have made the English-speaking people the foremost of the world. The distinguishing trait of our German ancestors was the individualism and independence of the citizen. With them the citizen was not the creature of government, but government was the creature of the citizen. The people were the fountain of political power, and rulers were their chosen servants. It was well said by Mr. JEFFERSON, when he proposed the figures of HENGIST and HORSA for the great seal of the United States, that they were " the Saxon chiefs from whom we claim the honor of being descended, and whose political principles and form of government we have assumed."

While Spain, France, and Italy were equally conquered by the Germans, their religion, social life, and administrative order remained Roman, and the conquerors became assimilated with the conquered. The result was peoples dominated by the Latin race. But in England the result was far different; there the Roman organization of government and society disappeared with the people that used it, and a purely German nation rose in its stead, a nation whose vitality was sufficient to absorb and assimilate the Danes and the Normans that in succession conquered the island. For more than one thousand years before the discovery of America this people advanced in civilization in their isolated island home. Within a century and a half from the landing of HENGIST upon the isle of Thanet, on the coast of England, AUGUSTINE, with a band of monks, landed on the same spot, and introduced Christianity, which soon supplanted the worship of Oden and gave a new and powerful impulse to the advancement of the nation. In the fifteenth century, when the light of the new learning broke upon the darkness of the Middle Ages, it shone on no land with greater luster than on England, nor with greater practical effects. One of the results of the mental activity which this revival of learning stirred in Europe was the daring voyage of Columbus in search of a new passage to the Indies, which led to the discovery of America. The sovereigns of Spain, who fitted out his fleet, claimed the New World as their possession. The Pope claimed the right to divide it between Spain and Portugal. For one hundred years the Spanish race were allowed to settle and occupy it at will, and during that time they demonstrated their unfitness to be its possessors. The same sovereigns who equipped the fleet of Columbus instituted that most cruel of all instruments of torture and rapacity, the Spanish Inquisition, and under its malign influence Spain attempted to stamp out Protestantism in Europe. It was with the same heartless cruelty and greed that the Spaniards murdered and robbed the natives of America, but their thirst for gold reacted on their own land in the neglect of the industries which lie at the basis of a nation's prosperity. At the end of the century the population of Spain had decreased four millions, while the great agricultural and commercial interests of the nation were in a visible decay. It was evident that God had something better in reserve for America than the Latin races of Europe, with their imperialism in church and state.

Separated from the continent, and developing along their own lines, yet absorbing what was best in Europe, the English had now become a great nation, under a noble constitution, in which local self-government

was happily blended with national authority, and personal liberty was made secure. The customs of their ancestors had crystallized into the common law, claimed to be the perfection of reason. The statute law had kept pace with the nation's growth, and that which was most valuable in the Roman civil law had been incorporated into their system.

The Great Charter, granted by King John the 15th of June, 1215, and frequently afterwards reaffirmed, had limited the power of the King and defined and guarded the rights of the citizen. The principle of representation of the people, peculiar to the Germans, had been developed, by which political power could be exercised over large areas without loss of vitality or danger of tyranny. The supreme power was exercised by Parliament, in which the chosen representatives of the people constituted the House of Commons; the Lords, spiritual and temporal, sat in the House of Lords; and the consent of the two houses, with that of the King, was necessary for the enactment of laws. Courts, presided over by learned judges, construed the law and administered justice. Every citizen was entitled to the shield of the law as a protection to his person and his property, and he enjoyed all the freedom that was compatible with the necessary powers of government.

In comparing the English system of government with that of other nations, MONTESQUIEU, the great Frenchman, was constrained to say that "the English is the only nation in the world where political and civil liberty is the direct end of its constitution."

It is true that tyrannical kings were prone to disturb the equilibrium of this well-balanced constitution, but the strong attachment of the people to their free institutions sooner or later restored it to its proper state, and the tyrants were made to know that the people were vested with the supreme power.

But the English people were not yet prepared to enter upon the theater of the New World, on which they were destined to play so grand a part. One thing was yet wanting to fit them for the heritage which had been prepared for them during the ages, and that came in the great reformation of the church which resulted from the revival of learning and the translation of the Bible. By the end of the sixteenth century the doctrines of the Reformation had pervaded England, and soon it could be said that the English had become the people of one book, and that book the Bible. Its translation constitutes the noblest example of the English tongue, and from its first appearance it became the standard of the language. It was eagerly read by the people, and they endeavored to shape their lives by its pure precepts. A great Puritan movement began, and had gathered immense volume, when the far-seeing RALEIGH, the most accomplished man of his day, infused into the nation his own enthusiasm for the scheme of planting an English nation in the part of North America not occupied by the Spaniards. The colonists came not to rob and murder the natives, but with a desire to Christianize them and to plant English institutions in the virgin soil of the New World. Old RICHARD HAKLUYT expressed the conviction of the English people when he wrote, " God hath reserved the countrys lying north of Florida to be reduced into Christian civility by the English nation."

In due course of time thirteen English colonies were firmly established along the Atlantic coast, but not without constant struggles with the French, who had settled on the north and west, and the Spaniards on the south, who with their Indian allies attacked them from their several quarters. But Providence had decreed to the English the possession of North America, and they could not be crushed nor their limits reduced. The victory of WOLFE at Quebec in 1759 and the subsequent treaty of Paris of 1763 destroyed the French power in North America, gave Canada to the English, and extended the western boundaries of the Colonies to the Mississippi. Thus the way was opened for the Colonies, when they became independent States, to extend their possessions to the Pacific and to fulfill the manifest destiny of the English race on this continent.

It was a century and a half after their first planting before the Colonies were sufficiently developed in population, in wealth, and in free institutions to assume for themselves the great trust which awaited them.

At their planting they brought with them the rights and privileges of Englishmen, secured by their charters. Separated from the mother country by a wide ocean, only to be crossed by tedious and dangerous voyages, local self-government sprang up and entered upon a vigorous growth. County or township government was copied, with improvements, from county government in England. Assemblies, elected upon a broad basis of suffrage, were the faithful representatives of the people and guardians of their rights, while the governors and councils, in imitation of king and lords, were united with the assemblies in the enactment of laws. A supervisory control was retained by the English Government, but in practice was seldom exercised. And thus the English Colonies were left, in their isolated condition, to their natural development, directed by the race characteristics of the people and

their new surroundings. These conduced to the formation of a noble manhood. The people were in the main agricultural and lived on their farms. The task of subduing the earth and defending their homes against a treacherous and savage foe stimulated their courage and self-reliance, while they learned the lesson of individual freedom. The Bible taught them that every man was responsible for his conduct to his Maker. This necessitated individual freedom of action, and so a Divine sanction was given to the free institutions which they had inherited from their heathen ancestors.

The Great Charter, wrested from the weak and treacherous John, had been made impregnable by the statute of Edward I, which confirmed to Parliament the exclusive right of taxation. These two formed the solid basis of the English constitution. The statute was a bulwark of defense for the charter, for with the power of taxation in the possession of the representatives of the people the castle of their liberties was impregnable.

The colonists claimed the exclusive right of taxing themselves, through their assemblies, as they were not represented in Parliament; and in no part of the Kingdom was this right more highly valued or more closely guarded.

After the Colonies had become firmly rooted their growth was rapid, and their development in material wealth was truly wonderful. By the middle of the eighteenth century they numbered one-fourth of the population of the mother country, and had become rich and prosperous, contributing largely to the wealth of Great Britain by their commerce. They had also advanced in their ideas of free government far beyond what was entertained in England, and were not behind her in the education and intelligence of the people. There was a tolerance in religion which was not known in the mother country or in Europe, and which was one of the strongest inducements of the emigration which crowded the ships leaving the ports of the Old World.

It was now that Parliament, under the dictation of a weak but stubborn King, and in contravention of the English constitution, determined to tax the Colonies without the consent of their assemblies. They respectfully remonstrated, then vigorously protested, and finally took up arms in defense of the great bulwark of their liberties. God gave them the victory, and the dependent Colonies became independent States. In framing their State governments they had the advantage not only of their own experience but of the experience of the world, and most wisely did they use it. No great revolution was ever led by abler men or by purer patriots. Virginia was the first colony to assume independence, and her incomparable statesmen, following English precedent, framed a bill of rights setting forth the fundamental principles of her new government. This remarkable paper, the greatest of its kind ever penned, marked the growth of free institutions in America. It was copied more or less closely by the other States, and became the foundation of American government. Of it Mr. BANCROFT says:

The Virginia Bill of Rights formed the groundwork of American institutions. It announced governmental principles for all peoples for all time. It was the voice of Reason going forth to speak a new political world into being.

Magna Charta and the Bill of Rights of 1688 had been drawn by great statesmen, and had been accepted as the best presentation of the rights of freemen ever penned. But the Virginia Bill of Rights, drafted by GEORGE MASON, a Virginia farmer, while embodying all that was of permanent value in these two, far excelled them in the fullness and clearness with which it states the rights of freemen and the fundamental principles of a free State. Let us glance at its provisions, upon which has been built the fabric of American Government. The first four sections read as follows:

1. That all men are by nature equally free and independent, and have certain inherent rights of which, when they enter into a state of society, they can not, by any compact, deprive or divest their posterity, namely, the enjoyment of life and liberty, with the means of acquiring and possessing property, and pursuing and obtaining happiness and safety.

2. That all power is vested in, and consequently derived from, the people; that magistrates are their trustees and servants, and at all times amenable to them.

3. That government is, or ought to be, instituted for the common benefit, protection, and security of the people, nation, or community; of all the various

modes and forms of government that is best which is capable of producing the greatest degree of happiness and safety, and is most effectually secured against danger of maladministration; and that when any government shall be found inadequate or contrary to these purposes, a majority of the community hath an indubitable, inalienable, and indefeasible right to reform, alter, or abolish it, in such manner as shall be judged most conducive to the public weal.

4. That no man or set of men are entitled to exclusive or separate emoluments or privileges from the community but in consideration of public services, which not being descendible, neither ought the offices of magistrate, legislator, or judge to be hereditary.

These sections set forth in most appropriate language the fundamental principles of a free republic, and having been substantially reproduced a few weeks afterwards in the Declaration of Independence of the Continental Congress, they became the utterance of the continent. They annihilate at one blow royalty, aristocracy, and privileged class, and boldly proclaim the equality of men before the law, their natural right to freedom, and the sovereignty of the people.

The fifth section declares that the legislative and executive powers shall be separate and distinct from the judiciary, and should be confined to fixed periods, the vacancies to be filled by frequent, certain, and regular elections. This was a great advance upon the English constitution, under which the legislative department exercised judicial powers and the Parliamentary elections were subject to the will of the King. It also guarded the purity and independence of the judiciary, which are of such vital importance in any system of good government. The sixth, seventh, eighth, ninth, and thirteenth sections, securing freedom of elections, confining the power of suspending laws to the legislature, guarding the rights of persons accused of crime, and prohibiting standing armies in times of peace, were based upon the provisions of the English Bill of Rights of 1688, but were improvements upon them. They enlarged the right of suffrage and extended it to "all men having sufficient evidence of permanent common interest with and attachment to the community," and declared that no law is binding upon the people unless assented to through their representatives. They secured to the accused an open and speedy trial by an impartial jury, and provided that he shall not be forced to give evidence against himself nor be deprived of his liberty except by the law of the land or the judgment of his peers. They placed the defense of the state upon a trained militia, and made the military in all cases subordinate to the civil power. This last is the only proper and safe course in a free state. Great standing armies in times of peace are not only dangerous to the liberties of the people, but by withdrawing large bodies of men from the fields of industry and taxing those who remain in those fields for their support they retard the prosperity of the state.

The tenth, eleventh, twelfth, fourteenth, fifteenth, and sixteenth sections were invaluable additions to the English Bill of Rights. They prohibited general warrants of arrest; declared that jury trial should be held sacred in civil controversies; secured the freedom of the press as one of the greatest bulwarks of liberty; declared the right of the people to uniform government; that free government can only be preserved "by a firm adherence to justice, moderation, temperance, frugality, and virtue, and by frequent recurrence to fundamental principles," and that "religion, or the duty we owe to our Creator, and the manner of discharging it, can be directed only by reason and conviction, not by force or violence, and therefore all men are equally entitled to the free exercise of religion according to the dictates of conscience." Of these the most valuable is the last, divorcing church and state from their debasing union, which for centuries had brought unnumbered woes upon mankind. It was the first time that a state had ever placed religion on the ground which the Founder of Christianity had claimed for it, and the principle is now held to be the contribution of America to the science of government and the chief corner stone of our system. It has shed the richest blessings upon both church and state in America, and will be the watchword of an advancing civilization throughout the world.

Upon these fundamental principles written constitutions were framed by the States defining and limiting the powers of government and limiting the exercise of sovereign power by the people themselves, thus securing permanency to their republican form of government.

But soon another important step was taken in the development of our institutions. The war of the Revolution had forced the Colonies to unite in the defense of their common liberties. They had conducted their common affairs through a congress, without any articles of confederation, until near the close of the war, and the articles then adopted were but a league between sovereign States. The federal functions were to be exercised by the Congress, in which each State delegation counted but as one vote. The body had no real power over the States, and could only advise them. As has been well said:

It could ask the States for money, but could not compel them to give it; it could ask them for troops, but could not force them to heed the requisition; it could make treaties, but must trust the States to fulfill them; it could contract debts, but must rely upon the States to pay them.

Under such a system, after the pressure of war had been removed, there could be nothing but State jealousies, internal disorder, weakness, and finally disintegration. The patriots who had won freedom and independence saw this clearly, and within half a decade after the signing of the treaty of peace the Articles of Confederation were cast aside and a new union formed under the Federal Constitution.

This marks the beginning of our history as a nation, and is an era in the development of free institutions. The problem before the convention which framed the Federal Constitution was new and difficult indeed, and by many deemed insoluble. It was the creation of a nation out of the citizens of the several States without destroying the autonomy of the States. It was to divide the sovereign power between the nation and the States, so as to invest the nation with ample supreme powers to conduct national affairs, and to leave with the States enough of sovereignty to conduct State affairs. It was to cause both governments to operate directly on the citizen, invested with a double citizenship, without a conflict in his allegiance. It was to perpetuate republican governments for both the nation and the States, each supreme in its functions, and so firmly fixed in its allotted sphere that they would never clash. The able men who solved this problem were statesmen of the highest order as well as patriots of the greatest purity. They thought they understood clearly their work, but they builded better than they knew. The form of government that they constructed has excited the admiration of the world. It has stood every test in peace and in war, and under it a great and ever-growing nation has developed, which rejoices more and more, as the years roll around, in the incalculable blessings it secures.

In the structure of the Federal Government the same principles were adopted which lay at the foundation of the State governments. The three great departments, legislative, judicial, and executive, were made separate and distinct, the executive, however, retaining a conditional veto upon the legislative department. The legislature was made bicameral, the Senate representing the States equally, the House of Representatives the people proportionally. The judiciary was made an independent, coordinate branch of the Government, vested with power to pass upon the constitutionality of the laws, State and Federal, and to declare null and void such as were not in accordance with the Constitution. Thus the national and State governments were to be kept in their appropriate spheres. The Executive was charged with the execution of the laws, and was made responsible for his conduct. The treaty-making power was vested in him, only to be exercised with the consent of the Senate. The powers of the Government were enumerated and were ample for the great objects of its creation, which were stated to be "to form a more perfect union, to establish justice, insure domestic tranquillity, provide for the common defense, promote the general welfare, and secure the blessings of liberty to ourselves and to our posterity." It has been well said by an able writer on our Government that—

The framers of this Government set before themselves four objects essential to its excellence, namely:

Its vigor and efficiency. The independence of its departments (as being essential to the permanency of its form). Its dependence on the people. The security under it of the freedom of the individual.

The first of these objects they sought by creating a strong executive; the second, by separating the legislative, executive, and judicial powers from one another, and by the contrivance of various checks and balances; the third, by making all authorities elective, and elections frequent; the fourth, both by the checks and balances aforesaid, so arranged as to restrain any one department from tyranny, and by placing certain rights of the citizen under the protection of the written Constitution.

So jealous were the people of their personal liberty and so determined to have their rights secured that without delay they ingrafted upon the Constitution ten amendments, eight of them containing a bill of rights based upon the Virginia bill, and two of them more clearly defining the boundary between the Federal and State governments.

At the close of the civil war another step forward was taken in the amendments which abolished slavery and secured equal privileges and immunities to all citizens throughout the Union. Thus our free institutions have developed until, from the Lakes to the Gulf, and from the Atlantic to the Pacific, a nation of sixty-five millions of freemen rejoice in the liberty which constitutional republican government has assured to them. The ancients worshiped their divinities as the guardians of their states; we only bow to constitutional law as the guardian of our institutions, and, in the language of the eloquent RUFUS CHOATE, we can say, "We have built no national temples but the Capitol. We consult no common oracle but the Constitution."

When we entered the family of nations as a republic, it was predicted that our Government would be shortlived, but now the ablest

H. Mis. 211——5

writers point out elements of permanency in our institutions, chief among which is the devotion of our people to their form of government. Yes, to-day, freed from the fears felt by Mr. WEBSTER in 1851, we can repeat his noble words with increased emphasis:

> Be it known that on this day the union of the United States of America stands firm, that their Constitution still exists unimpaired, and with all its original usefulness and glory; growing every day stronger and stronger in the affections of the great body of the American people, and attracting more and more the admiration of the world.

Our forefathers trusted the permanency of the Government they founded to the virtue and intelligence of the people. Virtue and intelligence! Divine attributes given to man when he was made in the image of God! As the two cherubim, with outstretched wings, covered and guarded the holy oracle in which was deposited the Ark of the Covenant, so may these guard and protect our Constitution, in which has been deposited the priceless jewel of liberty, as it is transmitted from generation to generation, till time shall end. And filled with the patriotic spirit of our founders, may those who administer the Government come year by year to this Capitol, and by wisdom in counsel do continued honor to their memory in contributing to the happiness of this great people. Illustrious founders!

> Ages on ages shall your fate admire!
> No future day shall see your names expire
> While stands the Capitol, immortal dome!

At the conclusion of Mr. HENRY's oration, the Centennial Chorus sang "The Star-Spangled Banner," accompanied by the Marine Band, the vast multitude joining in the chorus with great effect.

President CLEVELAND then arose and said that he had the pleasure of introducing a distinguished gentleman to respond for "The United States Senate," the Vice-President of the United States, Hon. ADLAI E. STEVENSON, of Illinois.

THE VICE-PRESIDENT'S ADDRESS

Mr. STEVENSON was welcomed with prolonged applause as President CLEVELAND led him to the front of the platform, and spoke in a most earnest and impressive manner, as follows:

FELLOW-CITIZENS: This day and this hour mark the close of a century of our national history. No ordinary event has called us together. Standing in the presence of this august assemblage of the people, upon

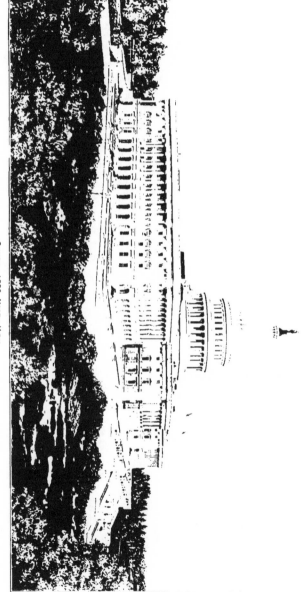

CAPITOL, 1893, NORTH VIEW.

the spot where WASHINGTON stood, we solemnly commemorate the one
hundredth anniversary of the laying of the corner stone of the nation's
Capitol.

It is well that this day has been set apart as a national holiday, that
all public business has been suspended, and that the President and his
Cabinet, the members of the great court and of the Congress, unite
with their countrymen in doing honor to the memory of the men who,
one hundred years ago, at this hour and upon this spot, put in place
the corner stone of the Capitol of the American Republic. The century
rolls back and we stand in the presence of the grandest and most
imposing figure known to any age or country. WASHINGTON, as
Grand Master of Free and Accepted Masons, clothed in the symbolic
garments of that venerable order, wearing the apron and the sash
wrought by the hands of the wife of the beloved LA FAYETTE, impress-
ively and in accordance with the time-honored usages of that order,
is laying his hands upon the corner stone of the future and permanent Capitol of his country. The solemn ceremonies of that hour
were conducted by WASHINGTON, not only in his office of Grand Master
of Free Masons, but in the yet more august office of President of the
United States. Assisting him in the fitting observance of these impressive rites were representatives of the Masonic lodges of Virginia and of
Maryland, while around him stood men whose honored names live with
his in history, the men who, on field and in council, had aided first in
achieving independence and then in the yet more difficult task of garner-
ing, by wise legislation, the fruits of victory. Truly the centennial of
an event so fraught with interest should not pass unnoticed.

History furnishes no parallel to the century whose close we now
commemorate. Among all the centuries it stands alone. With hearts
filled with gratitude to the God of our fathers, it is well that we recall
something of the progress of the young Republic since the masterful
hour when WASHINGTON laid his hands upon the foundation stone of
yonder Capitol.

The seven years of colonial struggle for liberty had terminated in
glorious victory. Independence had been achieved. The Articles of
Confederation, binding the Colonies together in a mere "league of
friendship," had given place to the Constitution of the United States,
that wonderful instrument, so aptly declared by Mr. GLADSTONE to be
"the most wonderful work ever struck off at a given time by the brain
and purpose of man."

Without a dissenting voice in the electoral college WASHINGTON
had been chosen President. At his council table sat JEFFERSON, the
author of the Declaration of Independence; HAMILTON, of whom it
has been said: "He smote the rock of the national resources, and
abundant streams of revenue gushed forth; he touched the dead corpse
of the public credit, and it sprang upon its feet;" KNOX, the brave

and trusted friend of his chief during the Colonial struggle, and
EDMUND RANDOLPH, the impress of whose genius has been indelibly
left upon the Federal Constitution. Vermont and Kentucky, as sovereign States, coequal with the original thirteen, had been admitted
into the Union. The Supreme Court, consisting of six members, had
been constituted, with the learned jurist, JOHN JAY, as its Chief Justice.
The popular branch of the Congress consisted of but one hundred and
five members. Thirty members constituted the Senate, over whose
deliberations presided the patriot statesman, JOHN ADAMS. The population of the entire country was less than four millions. The village
of Washington, the capital—and I trust for all coming ages the capital—contained but a few hundred inhabitants.

After peace had been con-
cluded with Great Britain,
and while we were yet under
the Articles of Confederation,
the sessions of the Congress
were held successively at Prince-
ton, Annapolis, Trenton, and New
York. In the presence of both
Houses of Congress, on the 30th day
of April, 1789, in the city of New
York, WASHINGTON had been inaugurated President. From that hour—
the beginning of our Government
under the Constitution—the Congress was held in New York until
1790, then in Philadelphia until 1800,
when, on November 17, it first convened in Washington. The necessity
of selecting a suitable and central place
for the permanent location of the seat of
government early engaged the thought-
ful consideration of our fathers. It can
not be supposed that the question reached a
final determination without great embarrassment, earnest discussion,
and the manifestation of sectional jealousies. But, as has been well
said, "the good genius of our system finally prevailed," and "a district of territory on the river Potomac, at some place between the
mouths of the Eastern Branch and the Connogacheague," was, by
act of Congress of June 28, 1790, "accepted for the permanent seat of
government of the United States."

From the 17th day of November, 1800, this city has been the capital.
When that day came WASHINGTON had gone to his grave JOHN

ADAMS was President, and JEFFERSON the presiding officer of the Senate. It may be well to recall that upon the occasion of the assembling for the first time of the Congress in the Capitol President ADAMS appeared before the Senate and the House, in joint session, and said:

It would be unbecoming the representatives of this nation to assemble for the first time in this solemn temple without looking up to the Supreme Ruler of the universe and imploring His blessing. You will consider it as the capital of a great nation, advancing with unexampled rapidity in arts, in commerce, in wealth and population, and possessing within itself those resources which, if not thrown away or lamentably misdirected, will secure to it a long course of prosperity and self-government.

To this address of President ADAMS the Senate made reply:

We meet you, sir, and the other branch of the National Legislature in the city which is honored by the name of our late hero and sage, the illustrious WASHINGTON, with sensations and emotions which exceed our power of description.

From the date last given until the burning of the Capitol by the British in 1814, in the room now occupied by the Supreme Court, in the north wing, were held the sessions of the Senate. That now almost forgotten apartment witnessed the assembling of Senators who, at an earlier period of our history, had been the associates of WASHINGTON and of FRANKLIN, and had themselves played no mean part in crystallizing into the great organic law the deathless principles of the Declaration of Independence. From this chamber went forth the second declaration of war against Great Britain, and here, before the Senate as a court of impeachment, was arraigned a justice of the Supreme Court of the United States to answer the charge of alleged high crimes and misdemeanors.

With the rolling years and the rapid growth of the Republic came the imperative necessity for enlarging its Capitol. The debates upon this subject culminated in the act of Congress of September 30, 1850, providing for the erection of the north and south wings of the Capitol. THOMAS U. WALTER was the architect to whose hands was committed the great work. Yonder noble structure will stand for ages the silent witness of the fidelity with which the important trust was discharged.

The corner stone of the additions was laid by President FILLMORE on the 4th day of July, 1851. In honor of that event, and by request of the President, Mr. WEBSTER pronounced an oration, and while we have a country and a language his words will touch a responsive chord in patriotic hearts. Beneath the corner stone was then deposited a paper in the handwriting of Mr. WEBSTER, containing the following words:

If it shall hereafter be the will of God that this structure shall fall from its base, that its foundation be upturned and this deposit brought to the eyes of men, be it then known that on this day the Union of the United States of America stands firm, that their Constitution still exists unimpaired, with all its original

usefulness and glory, growing every day stronger and stronger in the affections
of the great body of the American people, and attracting more and more the
admiration of the world. And all here assembled, whether belonging to public
life or to private life, with hearts devoutly thankful to Almighty God for the
preservation of the liberty and happiness of the country, unite in sincere and
fervent prayers that this deposit, and the walls and arches, the domes and
towers, the columns and entablatures now to be erected over it, may endure
forever.

From the 6th day of December, 1819, until January 4, 1859, a period
of thirty-nine years, the sessions of the Senate were held in the present Supreme Court room. This was indeed the arena of high debate.
When, in any age or in any country, has there been gathered within so
small compass so much of human greatness? To even suggest the

great questions here discussed and determined would be to write a history
of that eventful period. It was indeed
the coming together of the master
spirits of the second generation of American statesmen. Here were MACON
and CRAWFORD, BENTON, RANDOLPH,
CASS, BELL, HOUSTON, PRESTON,
BUCHANAN, SEWARD, CHASE, CRIT-
TENDEN, SUMNER, CHOATE, EVERETT,
BREESE, TRUMBULL, FESSENDEN,
DOUGLAS, CLAY, CALHOUN, WEBSTER,
and others scarcely less illustrious.
Within the walls of that little chamber was heard the wondrous debate
between HAYNE and WEBSTER. There
began the fierce conflict of antagonistic
ideas touching the respective powers of
the States and of the nation—a conflict
which, transferred to a different theater,
found final solution only in the bloody
arbitrament of arms.

For a little more than a third of a
century the sessions of the Senate have
been held in the magnificent chamber of the north wing of the Capitol. Of the procession of sixty-two Senators that, preceded by the
Vice-President, Mr. BRECKINRIDGE, entered that Chamber for the first
time on the 4th day of January, 1859, but four survive. Not one
remains in public life. It is indeed now a procession of shadows.

When the foundation stone of this Capitol was laid, our Republic
was in its infancy and self-government yet an untried experiment.
It is a proud reflection to-day that time has proved the true arbiter,

and that the capacity of a free and intelligent people to govern them selves by a written constitution and laws of their own making is no longer an experiment. The crucial test of a century of unparalleled material prosperity has been safely endured.

In 1793 there was no city west of the Alleghanies. To-day a single city on Lake Michigan contains a population of a little less than one-half that of the Republic at the time of the first inauguration of WASHINGTON. States have been carved out of the wilderness, and our great rivers, whose silence met no break on their pathway to the sea, are now the arteries of our interior trade, and bear upon their bosoms a commerce which surpasses a hundredfold that of the entire country a century ago.

From fifteen States and four millions of people we have grown to fifty States and Territories and sixty-seven million people; from an area of eight hundred and five thousand to an area of three million six hundred thousand square miles; from a narrow strip along the Atlantic seaboard to an unbroken possession from ocean to ocean. How marvelous the increase in our national wealth! In 1793 our imports amounted to $31,000,000 and our exports to $26,000,000. Now our imports are $847,000,000 and our exports $1,030,000,000. Thirty-three million tons of freight are carried on our Great Lakes, whose only burden then was the Indian's canoe. Then our national wealth was inconsiderable; now our assessed valuation amounts to the enormous sum of $24,650,000,000. Then trade and travel were dependent upon beasts of burden and sailing vessels; now steam and electricity do our bidding, railroads cover the land, boats burden the waters, the telegraph reaches every city and hamlet, distance is annihilated, and—

> Civilization, on her luminous wings,
> Soars, Phœnix-like, to Jove.

In the presence of this wondrous fulfillment of predicted greatness prophecy looks out upon the future and stands dumb.

When this corner stone was laid, France, then in the throes of revolution, had just declared war against Great Britain, a war in which all Europe eventually became involved. Within a century of that hour, in the capital of France, there convened an international court, its presiding officer an eminent citizen of the French Republic, its members representatives of sovereign European states, its object the peaceable adjustment of controversies between Great Britain and the United States.

Was it RICHELIEU, Mr. President, who said, " Take away the sword! States can be saved without it "?

In no part of our mechanism of government was the wisdom of our fathers more strikingly displayed than in the division of power into the three great departments—legislative executive, and judicial. In

an equal degree was that wisdom manifested by the division of the
Congress into a Senate and House of Representatives. Upon the Senate the Constitution has devolved important functions other than those
of a mere legislative character. Coequal with the House in matters
of legislation, it is, in addition, the advisory body of the President in
appointments to office and in treating with foreign nations. The
mode of election, together with the long term of service, unquestion-
ably fosters a spirit of conservatism in the Senate. Always organized,
it is the continuing body of our National Legislature. Its members
change, but the Senate continues the same now as at the first hour of
the Republic. Before no human tribunal come for determination issues

of weightier moment. It
were idle to doubt that
problems yet lie in our
pathway as a nation as
difficult of solution as any
that in times past have
tried the courage or tested
the wisdom of our fathers.

Yet may we not confi-
dently abide in the faith
that in the keeping of
those who succeed the
illustrious sages I have
named the dearest inter-
ests of our country will
be faithfully conserved,
and, in the words of an
eminent predecessor—

Though these marble walls
molder into ruin, the Senate,
in another age, may bear into
a new and larger chamber the
Constitution, vigorous and in-
violate, and that the last gen-
eration of posterity shall witness the deliberations of the representatives of
American States, still united, prosperous, and free.

And may—

Our fathers' God, from out whose hand
The centuries fall like grains of sand—

continue to the American people throughout all the ages the prosperity
and blessings which He has given to us in the past.

The Marine Band then played a potpourri of national airs
arranged by Professor FANCIULLI.

CAPITOL. 1893. NORTHEAST VIEW.

SPEAKER CRISP'S ADDRESS

President CLEVELAND then introduced, to respond for "The United States House of Representatives," CHARLES FREDERICK CRISP, Speaker of the House, who was received with cheer upon cheer.

Mr. CRISP said, turning to President CLEVELAND:

Mr. CHAIRMAN: When the corner stone of this great Capitol was laid, our Constitution was not six years old. Government by the people had barely reached the experimental stage. There were but fifteen States in the Union. Our population was less than four millions, and the House of Representatives, for which I now speak, was composed of only one hundred and five members. To-day, one hundred years thereafter, our Constitution still exists unimpaired; government by the people has been firmly established; our population exceeds sixty-seven millions, and the House of Representatives is composed of three hundred and fifty-six members.

During the century which has passed since WASHINGTON stood where we now stand, the world has watched with wonder and amazement the marvelous growth and development of our country. When that century began we were "weak in resources, burdened with debt, just struggling into political existence, and agitated by the heaving waves which were overturning European thrones." Its end finds us strong in resources, strong in wealth and credit, strong in numbers, and strong in the affection of an intelligent and united people. In all that constitutes real greatness the United States is to-day the foremost nation of the earth.

In behalf of all present I am sure I will be permitted to say we devoutly thank Almighty God for the wisdom and patriotism of the founders of our Government. We thank Him for the peace, the prosperity, the freedom, and the happiness of our people; and we do all most sincerely and fervently pray that our constitutional Union may endure forever.

The next musical number, "The Heavens are Telling," from the "Creation," was rendered by the Centennial Chorus, accompanied by the Marine Band.

JUSTICE BROWN'S ADDRESS

THE President then introduced Mr. Justice HENRY BILLINGS BROWN, of the Supreme Court of the United States, to respond for "The Judiciary."

Mr. BROWN said:

Mr. CHAIRMAN: This grand and beautiful building, whose centennial anniversary we are met to celebrate, was designed primarily as the official abode of the Congress of the United States, but from its completion to the present day it has also been the seat of its highest court. The judiciary act of 1789 required the sessions of the Supreme Court to be held at the seat of government, which was then the city of New York; and at the Exchange in that city, in February, 1790, the court was organized, and the judges, with Chief Justice JOHN JAY at their head, were sworn and qualified according to law. Nothing appears to have been done, however, beyond the appointment of subordinate officers and the entertainment of the court at an elaborate banquet (a feature religiously commemorated at its centennial in 1890), until the February term of 1791, when the court met in the south chamber of the city hall, in the city of Philadelphia, to which place the seat of government had been removed, and continued its sessions there until 1801, when it was finally transferred to Washington.

Its sessions in Philadelphia would not have been memorable but for the great case of Chisholm against the State of Georgia, in which the majority of the court held that an action would lie by an individual against a sovereign State of the Union. This case marked the beginning of a conflict between the Federal Government and the States which agitated the court for the next seventy years, and still occasionally engages its attention. By this generation, accustomed as it is to the prompt and cheerful acquiescence of the public in its decisions, the excitement created by this case can scarcely be realized. The State of Georgia not only denied its obligation to appear, protested against the jurisdiction of the court, and declined even to submit an argument in its own behalf, but refused to obey the judgment, and denounced the penalty of death against anyone who should presume to execute final process within its jurisdiction. The popular prejudice against the decision finally culminated in a constitutional amendment which practically nullified the judgment of the court and inhibited private actions against a State. Plain as this provision seems to be, this amendment, so far from putting at rest the stability of a State, has been pregnant with litigation to the present day.

The vigorous life of the Supreme Court may be said to have begun with the appointment of JOHN MARSHALL as Chief Justice, and the contemporaneous transfer of its sessions to a room in the basement of this Capitol, beneath the Chamber of the Senate. The court met here in August, 1801, and for the next sixty years, the most important in the history of the court, this vaulted and gloomy crypt continued to be its home. In this apartment were pronounced the great opinions which established the fame of MARSHALL as the expounder of the Constitution and the foremost jurist of the century. The Constitution had been adopted by the vote of the thirteen States of the Union, but its construction was a work scarcely less important than its original creation. With a large liberty of choice, guided by no precedents, and generally unhampered by his colleagues upon the bench, the great Chief Justice, determining what the law was by what he thought it ought to be, evolved, from his own experience of the defects of the Articles of Confederation and from an innate consciousness of what the country required, a theory of construction which time has vindicated and the popular sentiment of succeeding generations has approved. In the case of Marbury *v.* Madison, which arose at his very first term, he declared the judicial power to extend to the annulment of an act of Congress in conflict with the Constitution, a doctrine peculiar to this country, but so commending itself to the common sense of justice as to have been incorporated in the jurisprudence of every State in the Union. The lack of this check upon the action of the legislature has wrecked the constitution of many a foreign state, and it is safe to say that our own would not have long survived a contrary decision. Had MARSHALL rendered no other service to the country, this of itself would have been sufficient to entitle him to its gratitude.

The fame of MARSHALL rests upon less than thirty of his opinions. He rarely cited an authority, but the reasons he gave were so cogent that no amount of authority would have strengthened them. While his opinions lack the exhaustive research of Justice STORY'S, they surpass them in vigorous logic, and seem like the summing up and compendium of all prior adjudications upon the subject. His associates upon the bench were worthy compeers of such a man. Beside him sat BUSHROD WASHINGTON, a favorite nephew of the General; a man of small and emaciated frame, but a laborious student, sound in judgment, "clear in statement and learned in discussion;" a Federalist of the Marshall type and a judge "fearless, dignified, and enlightened," whose opinions have always commanded the respect of the profession. Here also sat WILLIAM PATERSON, who had been a Senator from New Jersey, and one of the authors of the famous judiciary act of 1789. Here, too, was STORY, who has been called the WALTER SCOTT of the common law, the foremost juridical writer of his age, a student whose passion for research halted not at the confines of the law of England and America, but embraced all that was accessible in the ancient and modern jurisprudence of continental Europe—an author whose works were as well known and much respected in Westminster Hall as in the court rooms of his native country. While his fame as a writer has eclipsed to a certain extent his labors as a judge, his opinion upon circuit in the case of De Lovio *v.* Boit is unsurpassed in learning and research, and may be justly said to have laid the foundations of our admiralty jurisprudence.

The bar was not less illustrious than the bench. At its head was EDMUND RANDOLPH, first Attorney-General of the United States, whose fearless conduct of the Chisholm case against the State of Georgia, unpopular as it was, elicited even the admiration of his enemies; WILLIAM PINCKNEY, the most eminent lawyer of his age, who united profundity of thought and brilliancy of expression to an extent never equaled, except possibly by RUFUS CHOATE; WILLIAM WIRT, the most persuasive orator of the bar, who argued against his native State the power of Congress to incorporate a bank; General WALTER JONES, pronounced by MARSHALL "the finest constitutional lawyer who ever argued a case before him;" DANIEL WEBSTER, then in the fullness of his intellectual vigor, pleading in a voice choked with emotion for the life of his alma mater, and later defending the Christian religion against an alleged stigma cast upon it in the will of STEPHEN GIRARD; DEXTER, of Massachusetts; HOFFMAN, OGDEN, and EMMET, of New York; INGERSOLL, SARGENT, and BINNEY, of Pennsylvania; MARTIN and HARPER, of Maryland, and a score of others scarcely less notable, who contributed to make of this the golden age of American oratory.

The first and what may be termed the Federalistic era of the Supreme Court terminated with the death of MARSHALL, in 1835. In a judicial career of thirty-four years he had so borne himself as not only to win the applause of his friends but the respect of his political opponents. He had not only settled the construction of the Constitution upon a broad and liberal basis, but he had immeasurably increased the importance of the court. From a tribunal of little apparent consequence he had raised it to the dignity of a coordinate branch of the Government.

It seems somewhat strange to the present generation that the first Chief Justice should have resigned to accept the governorship of New York, and have subsequently declined a reappointment because, to use his own language, he was "perfectly convinced that under a system so defective it would not obtain the energy, weight, and dignity which were essential to its affording due support to the National Government, nor acquire the public confidence and respect which, as the last resort of the justice of the nation, it should possess." The little esteem in which the court was held induced HARRISON, a nominee of WASHINGTON, to decline a seat upon the bench to take the chancel-

lorship of Maryland; and its removal to this city seemed of so little
importance that its first meeting and organization here were noticed
by only a single sentence in the National Intelligencer.

The death of MARSHALL was soon followed by the elevation of ROGER
B. TANEY to the Chief Justiceship, and an almost entire reconstruction
of the bench by JACKSON and VAN BUREN. This, which may be called
the States' rights era, continued until the middle of the civil war, when
the court was again partly reconstructed by President LINCOLN. While
Chief Justice TANEY went upon the bench staggering under a load of
unpopularity in the Whig States—an unpopularity which had once
caused his rejection by the Senate for the office of Associate Justice—
it must be conceded that he
was a worthy successor of
MARSHALL. Though
feeble in body, his intellectual grasp was
something won-
derful. He was
prompt and deci-
sive in action, vig-
orous in expression,
spotless in integ-
rity, and in his
manner the ex-
treme of courtesy.
While his person-
ality dominated the bench
for twenty-five years al-
most as completely as had that of
MARSHALL, he was supported by men
of distinguished ability and large expe-

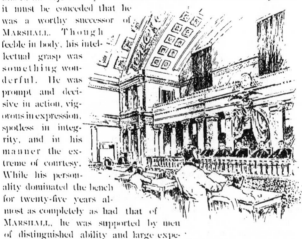

rience—JOHN McLEAN, of Ohio, whose dissenting opinion in the
great case of Prigg against the Commonwealth of Pennsylvania, read
after the lapse of fifty years, makes us wonder the majority of the
court could have gone so far astray; WAYNE, of Georgia, and CATRON,
of Tennessee, who earned at least the gratitude of the North for
their resolute adherence to the Union after the outbreak of the civil
war; PETER V. DANIEL, of Virginia, the strongest champion of States'
rights who ever sat upon the bench, a man of great learning, sturdy
independence, and strict integrity, who devoted a long judicial life of
nineteen years largely to the writing of dissenting opinions; NELSON,
of New York, of venerable and leonine aspect; GRIER, of Pennsylvania, who had well earned the compliment paid him by President
GRANT upon his retirement, that by his patriotic firmness he had
"upheld the just powers of the Government and vindicated the right

of the nation to maintain its own existence:" BENJAMIN R. CURTIS, of Massachusetts, one of the greatest minds that ever adorned the bench, who would have been the most eminent judge of the court if he had not resigned after a service of six years to become its most eminent practitioner.

In 1860, after the removal of the Senate to its new Chamber in the north wing of the Capitol, the Supreme Court was transferred to the room it now occupies. This room, beautiful in itself, and made more beautiful by the removal of the galleries which had encircled its walls, had already become historic as the theater of the greatest forensic displays of an age when oratory had still preserved its classic traditions and had lost nothing of its potency as a moving power of legislative bodies. But the great men of that generation were no longer there. WEBSTER, CLAY, CALHOUN, BENTON, and WRIGHT were all dead, and a new generation of Senators had risen up to take their places. The days of eloquent appeal, fierce denunciation, and heated strife were past. Henceforth this Chamber was dedicated to the calm deliberations of the bench.

The third era of the Supreme Court, which continues to this day, may be said to have begun in 1862 with the appointment of Justices SWAYNE, MILLER, and DAVIS, and the subsequent elevation of CHASE to the Chief Justiceship. This era, too, has been productive of great judges. Time forbids that I should do more than mention the name of CHASE, whose laurels as the great War Secretary were not dimmed by his service upon the bench; of WAITE, the very ideal of an accomplished lawyer and courtly gentleman; of MILLER, whose massive head did not belie his massive intellect, and whose fame as a constitutional lawyer is second only to that of the great Chief Justice; of MATTHEWS, a patriotic soldier, a Senator of the United States, and the most eloquent orator of the court; of the chivalrous LAMAR, whose kindly smile and genial manner captivated the hearts of men and women alike; of BRADLEY, who concealed beneath the visage of an Italian cardinal the most marvelous versatility of genius, a lawyer equally at home in all branches of the profession, real estate, mining, patents, equity, admiralty, and the civil law, a linguist, a mathematician, an astronomer, and a philosopher; and the lamented BLATCHFORD, painstaking and indefatigable, who loved work for its own sake, and whom the allurements of an ample fortune could not seduce from his chosen field of labor.

It is invidious to speak of the living, yet I can not forbear alluding to the venerable survivor of that illustrious trio who for more than twenty years swayed the opinion of the court; one who sits with us to-day, his eye not yet dimmed nor his natural force abated, a reminder of what the court has been in the past, a promise of what it shall continue to be in the future.

It does not become me to eulogize the Supreme Court, but it may be justly said that while it has had weak men history makes no mention of its having had a corrupt one.

If as at present constituted it neglects to fulfill its mission it will not be from a failure of its members to fully appreciate their responsibility or the lack of an earnest desire to meet the just expectations of the people.

I can not better close than by reiterating the hope expressed by the House of Representatives in its reply to President ADAMS upon the dedication of this building, that—

The spirit which animated the great founder of this city may descend to future generations, and that the wisdom, magnanimity, and steadiness which mark the events of his public life may be imitated in all succeeding ages.

Next on the programme was the "Centennial March," composed by Professor FANCIULLI for the occasion, and rendered by the full Marine Band with exquisite effect.

COMMISSIONER PARKER'S ADDRESS

After the applause with which the music was received had somewhat subsided, President CLEVELAND announced that "The District of Columbia" would be responded for by Mr. MYRON M. PARKER, one of the Board of Commissioners of the District of Columbia, Mr. JOHN W. ROSS, President of the Board of Commissioners of the District of Columbia, having been prevented by an accident from making preparation for that duty.

Mr. PARKER, turning toward Mr. CLEVELAND, said:

Mr. CHAIRMAN: The ceremonies that are transpiring here to-day will occupy an important page in the history of our country. The celebration of the one hundredth anniversary of the laying of the corner stone of the United States Capitol will be of unusual interest to the people of our land, while to the citizens of Washington it is an event of more than local importance, since it will emphasize our wondrous growth and greatness. All Governments point with pride to their respective capitals. To speak of London is to refer to England; the name of Paris covers that of France. If you would refer to Austria, you have only to mention Vienna; while Rome, with her eternal hills, overshadows Italy. So, too, of our own beloved country, a unification of States, with a rapidly increasing population of sixty-five millions of people, every one of whom is thrilled with pride and patriotism at the mention of Washington, their beautiful capital.

The application of these proceedings from an executive, legislative, and judicial standpoint has been appropriately considered by the President and Vice-President of the United States, by the honorable Speaker of the House of Representatives, and by Mr. Justice BROWN, of the Supreme Court; and from a national standpoint in an eloquent address by the Hon. WILLIAM WIRT HENRY, of Virginia. It is fitting, therefore, that as one of the Commissioners of the District of Columbia I should speak of the event which these imposing ceremonies commemorate with respect to the influences which have resulted to the city of Washington locally. To properly discuss this subject would occupy much more than the time allotted me by the Committee. I must therefore refer briefly to some of the material points.

The location of the national capital was a subject of much contention between the North and the South. Claimants for the honor of provid-

ing a permanent seat of government were made unyielding in their demands by State pride and State jealousy. Sectional animosities also added to the bitterness of the controversy.

Congress found this subject a fruitful source of wrangling. This body met in different places, according as convenience suggested or necessity compelled, naming from time to time different locations, only to reverse its decision at the next discussion of the subject. It will be remembered that the proposed site on the Potomac, supported by many Southern members, was repeatedly rejected.

In 1783 a location on the Delaware was thought more desirable than the one on the Potomac, and in 1784 Congress appointed a commission to select a site upon the former river.

That this selection was not made is well known to the country, and the contention was left to the first Congress meeting under the Constitution. Upon the meeting of this body the wrangle became more heated than ever before. Philadelphia, Germantown, Havre de Grace, Wrights Ferry, on the Susquehanna, and a location on the Potomac were each urged as having the strongest claims.

The persistency of Mr. MADISON and other Southern members finally prevailed, and in July, 1790, the House, by a vote of thirty-two to twenty-nine, and the Senate, by a vote of fourteen to twelve, decided in favor of the Potomac.

After years of preparation for the event, during which period the site was selected by President WASHINGTON, work on the several buildings was begun, and Washington, as the nation's capital, came into being.

Since 1800, the date on which the archives of the Government were brought from Philadelphia in "seven large boxes and four or five smaller ones," there have been periodical attempts to remove the seat of government, which removal would, of course, have been the death knell of Washington. An Englishman named WELD, who visited the future capital in 1796, said:

Notwithstanding all that has been done at the city and the large sums of money which have been expended, there are numbers of people in the United States living to the north of the Potomac, particularly in Philadelphia, who are still very adverse to the removal of the seat of government thither, and are doing all in their power to check the progress of the buildings in the city and to prevent the Congress from meeting there at the appointed time.

A sample of the attacks upon the capital may be found in CRITO'S Letters on the Seat of Government, published in 1807. He says:

In the meantime be it known to the good people of the Union from New Hampshire to Georgia (for I may presume without fear of contradiction that ninety-nine hundredths of the youth of the United States grow up to manhood without ever having seen the capital of their country; that the national bantling called the city of Washington remains, after ten years of expensive fostering, a rickety infant, unable to go alone. Nature will not be forced. A sickly child can not be dressed and dandled into a healthy constitution. This embryo of the state will always be a disappointment to its parents, a discredit to the fond opinions of its worthy godfathers and godmothers, and an eyesore to all its relations to the remotest degree of consanguinity.

CRITO concludes his advice by recommending that the seat of government be removed to Philadelphia.

The last attempt to remove the capital was made in 1869 by L. U. REAVIS and others, in and out of Congress, St. Louis being the city that was to become the future capital. Mr. REAVIS, in his book, says:

I unhesitatingly answer that the change will be made within five years from January 1, 1869, and before 1875 the President of the United States will deliver his message at the new seat of government in the Mississippi Valley.

There were many influences about this time which tended to check and finally to wipe out all efforts having in view the removal of the capital.

Under the leadership of a man of high character, great executive ability and determination, a man with broad, comprehensive views, a system of public improvements was inaugurated and carried to a successful conclusion which so changed the character and condition of our city as to place it at the beginning of a new era, an era of prosperity which in an unprecedented manner has continued to exist and which

H. Mis. 211——6

will continue to exist so long as the Government lasts. As Baron HAUSSMANN was to Paris so was Governor SHEPHERD to Washington. Under his guiding hand a new city was born, the hopes of the immortal WASHINGTON and L'ENFANT were realized, and Washington was finally accepted by the people of the United States as the national capital, the nation's home.

Let us look for a moment at the physical conditions of the city up to 1875. CHARLES W. JANSEN, an Englishman, said of us in 1806:

Strangers, after viewing the offices of state, are apt to inquire for the city while they are in its very center.

OLIVER WOLCOTT, while Secretary of the Treasury, and Mrs. President ADAMS complained of the scattered condition of the houses. In 1814, after the Secretary of War had sneered at the suggestion that the British might molest the "Sheep-walk," and after the national representatives, more than our own local defenders, had permitted the city to be captured, it had the following appearance:

Twelve or fifteen clusters of houses, at a considerable distance from each other, bringing to our recollection the appearance of a camp of nomad Arabs, which, however, if connected together, would make a very respectable town, not much inferior, perhaps, to the capital of Virginia, the whole of it, when seen from the ruins of our public edifices, looking more like the place where proud Washington once stood than where humble Washington now lies.

In 1839, GEORGE COMBE, the British traveler, described the city as "like a large straggling village reared in a drained swamp."

At about this period our corporation laws prohibited hogs from running at large "south of Massachusetts avenue" under penalty of seizure. All the land north of that avenue was free pasturage. As late as 1862, speaking of Massachusetts avenue, ANTHONY TROLLOPE says:

Massachusetts avenue runs the whole length of the city, and is inserted on the maps as a full-blown street about four miles in length. Go there and you will find yourself not only out of town, away among the fields, but you will find yourself beyond the fields, in an uncultivated wilderness. Tucking your trousers up to your knees, you will wade through the bogs, you will lose yourself among rude hillocks, you will be out of the reach of humanity.

Let us contrast this truthful description of thirty years ago with the present Massachusetts avenue, lined on either side with magnificent residences, and we can reach a fair conclusion of the phenomenal growth and prosperity of Washington. The Congress of the United States selected Washington and laid it out on a magnificent scale, the wisdom of which has been justified by the experience of a century. So broad and comprehensive was this plan that our people found themselves almost in a condition of bankruptcy in their effort, unaided by the General Government, to erect buildings and improve streets.

CAPITOL, 1893, NORTHWEST VIEW.

We find, therefore, that after much wrangling and contention the capital was located on the Potomac, in a comparative wilderness, and abandoned by the General Government so far as financial aid was concerned.

Congress, while liberal in the expenditure of the people's money, declined to appropriate money to make the national capital attractive. For years the capital intrusted to its keeping continued to be an object of derision and contempt. Aye, more than that—it contributed by its own neglect to make more wretched the city's forlorn condition, and then joined in the laugh at the latter's expense.

Finding this to be the unhappy condition, let me occupy a moment of your time with a brief statement of what our city has done for itself and the General Government.

First, it must be remembered that the United States owns one-half of all the property in the District, on which it pays no taxes, and prior to 1878 it never contributed anything for the support of our local government.

When the capital was located in Washington our citizens donated five-sevenths of all the land in the city of Washington for streets and avenues—fifty-four per cent of the entire area for parks and reservations, or five hundred and forty-one acres. One-half of all the city lots were given to help erect public buildings and to open and improve streets. Up to 1835 the citizens (the population at that time had only reached thirteen thousand) had expended for street improvements, mostly around public buildings, $430,000; the United States, $209,000. From 1790 to 1878, almost a century, the Government expended (aside from public buildings) less than $6,000,000; the citizens, $45,000,000. From 1879 to 1887 our people invested in new buildings $32,000,000. They paid a direct tax of $20,000 for the war of 1812, fitted up a building for Congress when the Capitol was burned, and tendered a loan of $500,000 to rebuild the public buildings, which Congress accepted. During the last war we paid a direct tax of $50,000. We have paid an internal-revenue tax of $6,454,907, and in one year twice as much as any of the Territories, except Dakota, and more than either of the States of Alabama, Arkansas, Maine, Mississippi, Nevada, South Carolina, or Vermont.

We supplied our share of volunteers for the war of 1812 and the Mexican war. In the late war we furnished our full quota and eighteen and one-half per cent over, while but seven States filled their quota and only one equaled the District. In the late war the first volunteers were citizens of the District.

The Government has given to the States $28,000,000 in money, 90,000,000 acres of public lands for schools and 155,000,000 acres for railroads. The District of Columbia has never been given a dollar or an acre of ground.

It must not be thought that we do not appreciate the benefits that have resulted from the millions that have been expended by the Government in the erection of public buildings, nor are we unmindful of the fact that since 1878 the Government has borne her share of the expenses; but we do claim that Washington has done far more for herself and the General Government than should have been expected by Congress.

We have had three different forms of government. From January 23, 1791, to June 1, 1802, the local government was vested in a board of three Commissioners appointed by the President. From 1802 to 1812 the Mayor was appointed by the President. From 1812 to 1820  the Mayor was elected by the Aldermen and Common Council. In 1871 the government was changed to Territorial in form and so continued until 1874, first HENRY D. COOKE and later ALEXANDER R. SHEPHERD having been appointed governors by the President. Congress, in 1874, again changed our government to a board of three Commissioners to be appointed by the President. This form of government is now in force, and is believed to be the best municipal form of government in existence. Under its provisions we are free from political broils and entanglements. Those who have been selected for the high and responsible position of Commissioners have been men of high character, every dollar contributed by our taxpayers and the General Government having been religiously accounted for. The government of the District of Columbia is free from even the suspicion of jobbery.

Our population in 1796 was 1,493; in 1860, 75,080; while to-day we number about 280,000.

Since June 11, 1878, Congress has appropriated annually fifty per cent of the approved estimates for expenditures of the District, the remaining fifty per cent being raised by taxation on the property.

The relations between the people of the District and Congress have been strengthened and unified from year to year. We are no longer regarded as mendicants, and our treatment is liberal and in keeping with the progress and dignity of the capital of a great republic.

From a wretched beginning Washington has grown to be the fairest and most attractive city in the land, and is recognized as one of the most beautiful in the world. We have upward of two hundred and fifty miles of smooth asphalted streets, fringed on either side by the luxurious and welcome shade of overhanging trees. Great national parks environ the city. Under the provisions of a recent act of Congress the magnificent plan of Washington will be continued and our broad streets and avenues will soon touch the District line. Years ago the rim of Washington was knocked off by our rapidly increasing population; Boundary street has been wiped out; our limits are now the boundaries of the District.

The broad waters of the Potomac flow on to the ocean kissing the silent, sacred shores of Mount Vernon. As all roads are said to have led to Rome, so do all avenues of culture lead to Washington.

Our public and private schools are unsurpassed. Already we have become a great literary, art, and scientific center. Universities representing different denominations have been and are being founded, with such unusual advantages as to attract the youth from all sections of our land. The capital, our climate, our city, our people, the advantages which result from the fostering care of the Government, such as the National Museum, collections of natural history, a Government library, models representing the inventive genius of a century, the Congress of the United States, the diplomatic representatives of the nations of the earth, all conspire to attract to us the cultured, the influential, the wealthy people of the world.

It would be impossible to overestimate our future possibilities. Our growth and prosperity will be an evidence and a result of national progress and greatness. No people are more loyal, generous, and hospitable than ours; no city on the face of the earth more attractive.

The District's second century will be but an echo of national advancement. We have already more than realized the fondest hopes of our founders; Washington is the ideal city of the world.

The day ceremonies at the Capitol then closed with the singing of "America," the Centennial Chorus being accompanied by the

Marine Band, and the multitude joining in the singing with great enthusiasm. The volume of sound from the voices of the thousands present was such as had never been heard before on any similar occasion.

NIGHT CONCERT

The night of September 18, 1893, was dark, but the arches of gas jets in front of the great white building threw a glare of light over the grand stands, gleaming upon the scarlet uniforms of the Marine Band and over the Centennial Chorus, which occupied the south stand.

At 6 o'clock the Centennial Chimes of thirteen bells rang out clearly and distinctly the evening programme heretofore given. During the pealing of the chimes the crowd had begun to collect at the east front of the Capitol, and when 8 o'clock arrived, the hour for the opening of the grand out-of-door night concert, the stands were filled to their utmost capacity, while, in the language of the newspapers of the day—

The whole of the open space before the east front of the Capitol was filled with a closely packed mass of humanity that extended out  over the grass plots back of the Greenough statue and north and south past the broad steps of the House and Senate wings. A sight of the great crowd from the lower gallery of the dome conveyed some idea of what is meant by "a sea of heads." Two-thirds of the way across the plaza one could have walked on the heads of the crowd with no danger of falling through a chance opening. Then came a great semicircle of closely packed carriages, and beyond that again, swarming over the grass plots, packed in tiers over the great ornamental urns, on the coping wall, and into East Capitol street, stretched the crowd.

It was shortly after 8 o'clock when the first strains of Professor FANCIULLI's grand march, "The National Capitol Centennial," rendered with exquisite accuracy, floated upon the still night. The great building, acting as a giant sounding-board, gave back the echoes, throwing the sound far out across the open space.

The Centennial Chorus, who were present to the full number of fifteen hundred, then sang "The Heavens Are Telling." The chorus was in fine voice and sang well together under the magnetic leadership of Professor CLOWARD, the clear notes of the sopranos

being distinctly heard by persons on the upper tier of the dome of the Capitol, nearly three hundred feet distant. The vast audience appreciated the grand music, and as the last notes of the chorus died away, broke out in prolonged cheers.

The Marine Band then rendered the overture from "Semiramide," and were followed by the Centennial Chorus in "Home,

Sweet Home," accompanied by the Marine Band. Then it was that the enthusiasm of the crowd was made manifest by cheer on cheer, which continued as the Marine Band played FANCIULLI'S merry descriptive music, "A Trip to Manhattan Beach."

The Centennial Chorus, accompanied by the Marine Band, and at times by the audience, then sang "Hail Columbia," the enthusiastic multitude insisting upon an encore, and being rewarded by the Marine Band with "Dixie," which was welcomed with alternate cheers and yells of delight.

The Marine Band then played ORTH'S "In the Clock Store," at the conclusion of which there was a mighty shout for "HANFORD! HANFORD!" As the actor, Mr. CHARLES B. HANFORD, appeared on the projecting pier to the south of the main steps the applause was deafening. Waving his hand to command silence, in a clear, deep voice, thrilling with emotion, Mr. HANFORD began to recite "The Star-Spangled Banner." Never had he recited to such a vast multitude, and never had he voiced or acted the stirring song so well. Cheers answered the closing lines of each verse, and at the close of the poem, as he raised aloft and waved to and fro a silken flag—the Star-Spangled Banner—the cheering became a deafening roar. Then the leader of the chorus waved his baton and the entire chorus and the thousands present in the crowd joined in singing the national air, while Mr. HANFORD stood far above the heads of the mass, waving time with the silken flag The demonstration of popular enthusiasm was mighty—"the voice of the American people."

The concert closed with "A Trip to Mars," one of FANCIULLI'S sprightly and entertaining compositions, which the Marine Band rendered with fine effect.

The Joint Committee

CAPITOL, 1893, WEST FRONT.

The Joint Committee

In pursuance of the joint resolution of Congress, the following Senators, Representatives, and citizens were appointed to serve on the Joint Committee, namely:

By the Senate:

DANIEL W. VOORHEES.
JOHN SHERMAN.
MATT W. RANSOM.

STEPHEN M. WHITE.
WILLIAM E. CHANDLER.
WATSON C. SQUIRE.

JOHN MARTIN.

By the House:

WILLIAM D. BYNUM.
JOHN C. BLACK.
DAVID B. HENDERSON.

JOHN DE WITT WARNER.
GEORGE W. HOUK.
CHARLES O'NEILL.

WILLIAM COGSWELL.

By the Citizens' Committee:

LAWRENCE GARDNER.
DUNCAN S. WALKER.
E. B. HAY.
M. I. WELLER.
C. C. GLOVER.
S. W. WOODWARD.
JOHN W. ROSS.

H. L. BISCOE.
B. H. WARNER.
A. R. SPOFFORD.
J. M. TONER.
JOHN JOY EDSON.
BERIAH WILKINS.
MARSHALL W. WINES.

The committee met in the rooms of the Senate Committee on Finance at 10 a. m., August 23, 1893, and, a quorum being present, organized with Hon. DANIEL WOLSEY VOORHEES, United States Senate, as Chairman, and General DUNCAN S. WALKER as Secretary.

After the reading of the joint resolution creating the committee, Chairman VOORHEES called upon the Chairman of the Citizens' Committee for a statement of what had been done by the Citizens' Committee in preparing for the celebration, and what was proposed to be done to carry into effect the joint resolution of Congress.

91

Chairman GARDNER submitted a written report, as follows:

At the request of the Citizens' Committee, the following report has been prepared for the information of the committee appointed from the Senate and House of Representatives, explaining the origin of the movement, what has been done, and what yet remains undone.

Being requested by numerous citizens, the District Commissioners issued a call through the daily papers, and a meeting was held accordingly at Willard's Hotel on June 7, at which meeting the Hon. JOHN W. Ross, President of the Board of Commissioners of the District of Columbia, presided. It was determined then to have an appropriate celebration, and Chairman Ross was delegated by the meeting to appoint a committee of fifty to conduct the affair. Mr. Ross appointed a committee which subsequently met at Willard's Hall and selected its officers, and it further empowered the Chairman to appoint such com-

mittees as were necessary to carry the celebration to a success. The committees were all appointed and their duties defined. It is unnecessary to state the details worked out by each committee. The result of the work done by and approved by the General Committee is as follows:

It might be well to state here that at the time the Citizens' Committee was appointed, and after it had completed the many arrangements for a great part of its programme, it was not anticipated that the Congress of the United States would be in session, and authority was procured from the Honorable the President of the Senate (there being no Speaker of the House of Representatives), under the act of Congress approved July 1, 1882, for the suspension of the prohibition of the use of the grounds, etc., so as to enable the celebration to be conducted as proposed. As soon as Congress met the matter was brought to its attention by the Citizens' Committee, and the Joint Committee was appointed at its request.

Under these circumstances we trust that it may not be regarded as presumptuous on our part to have already almost completed the arrangements, and that what has been done will meet with your approval.

A Committee on Ceremonies at the Capitol, under the direction of Mr. B. H. WARNER, have in part completed their programme. The portion that is absolutely concluded is as follows:

Prayer by Right Rev. WILLIAM PARET, Bishop of Maryland; introduction of the President; address by the President of the United States, introducing the orator, Mr. WILLIAM WIRT HENRY, of Richmond, Va and the following portion of the programme is respectfully suggested for action and approval: An address on behalf of the United States Senate, by its President; an address on behalf of the House of Representatives, by its Speaker; an address by a member of the Supreme Court, Chief Justice FULLER; an address for the District of Columbia, by one of the Commissioners of the District.

In presenting this programme the committee found it necessary to arrange for music, and their music committee has undertaken the task of securing and drilling one of the largest choruses ever brought together in the District of Columbia, consisting of fifteen hundred trained adult voices. At proper places during the programme the chorus will render patriotic music, concluding with a grand Te Deum. The committee has kindly had placed at its disposal a fine chime of thirteen bells, which will be rung at stated intervals during the day and in conjunction with the chorus. The committee has also secured the services of the United States Marine Band, which, at the cost of the committee, has arranged to increase its numbers. In preparing for the accommodation of this large number of musicians the committee has entered into a contract for the building of a stand at the side of the center steps at the east front of the Capitol that will accommodate twelve to thirteen hundred. They also arranged for a stand directly in front of the steps, for the accommodation of the President, speakers, and invited guests, perhaps to the number of about two hundred, which leaves the steps back of that stand yet free, to be used for other invited guests. If the Senate and House of Representatives desire to be present, it will be necessary to erect another stand on the opposite side of the center steps for their accommodation. To decorate the stands the committee would request that permission be secured from Congress for the War and Navy Departments to loan such flags and decorations as they may have.

It is proposed further that the event be celebrated by a parade, to march over the same route traveled by the procession in 1793. From such old records as we have been able to find, we learn that the procession assembled at the President's Square and marched thence to the Capitol grounds. An advertisement was published in the daily papers of the city inviting all military and civic organizations and associations in the District of Columbia and neighboring cities to participate in the parade and be present at the ceremonies. An additional written invitation was sent to such civic and military organizations whose addresses we could secure. In nearly all instances the invitations have been responded to, expressing a desire to participate in the parade, and only in one or two cases have we received declinations.

General ALBERT ORDWAY, commanding the District militia, has been selected by the committee as Grand Marshal. He is now hard at work with the Committee on Parade, arranging all the details.

Specially engraved invitations to the number of one thousand have been prepared. These invitations are to be sent to such prominent citizens of the United States as the committee may desire to invite, and also to the Diplomatic Corps. The design for the invitation is very elaborate, and tells the story of the building of the Capitol, beginning with a picture of President WASHINGTON laying the corner stone September 18, 1793; the second picture representing the old building completed, and the third representing the building as at present, 1893. Inclosed in the invitation are four pages, two pages to be devoted to the programme, one page containing the names of the Joint Committee, and the fourth page other committees.

The committee have also published a small pamphlet giving a history of the Capitol from its foundation up to the present time; it also contains a list of the committees appointed to date. We have only issued one thousand copies of the book, and the other two thousand are ready to be issued as soon as the programme is complete, so that the pamphlet will then contain the programme and any new committees, and such other information as will add to its historic value.

It is customary in celebrations of this kind to furnish the committee with ribbon badges, but the General Committee decided to have a medal struck commemorative of the occasion, designs for which were submitted and approved by the General Committee, and a contract for five hundred has been entered into, the medals to be paid for by the individual members of the committee. Facsimiles of the designs will be found on the front and back pages of the pamphlet.

It was first contemplated by the General Committee to have an evening entertainment at the Capitol, consisting of a reception in the Rotunda; but Congress being in session it was deemed advisable to abandon that portion of the programme.

After consultation with Architect CLARK, who, I may say here, has been of great service to this committee, his suggestions being always well timed, it was proposed to have an illumination of the Capitol building with electric lights; but, after correspondence, our committee found that it would be impossible to go into a matter of that kind in an appropriate way with the funds in hand. So at present all that is contemplated is an illumination of the dome, there being sufficient electric power at the Capitol to furnish us with all the current necessary. It was also proposed to use the grand festival chorus for a concert in the Capitol grounds on the evening of the 18th of September, having the grounds illuminated by gas and an aerial display of fireworks, the firing to take place from the grounds of the new

Library building; but as the committee has acted from the beginning on the principle of making no contracts except when the money was in hand, these matters are held in abeyance. We hope, however, to have an evening concert and an illumination of the grounds.

The additional legislation that this committee will require will be, first, a joint resolution granting us the use of the flags and decorations of the War and Navy Departments; second, a resolution making the 18th of September, 1893, a holiday for the District of Columbia.

The report of the Chairman of the Citizens' Committee was received and approved and the execution of the same placed in the hands of the Citizens' Committee.

It was also ordered that the Congress be requested to make the 18th day of September, 1893, a legal holiday in the District of Columbia, and also authorize the Secretary of War and the Secretary of the Navy to deliver to the Architect of the Capitol, for decoration purposes, certain ensigns, flags, and signal numbers.

Chairman GARDNER, of the Citizens' Committee, announced that his committee had raised by voluntary subscriptions the funds necessary for defraying all the expenses of the celebration.

The Joint Committee met in the rooms of the Finance Committee of the Senate September 11, at 10 a. m.; Senator DANIEL W. VOORHEES, Chairman, and General DUNCAN S. WALKER, Secretary.

Mr. GARDNER, Chairman of the Citizens' Committee, made the following report:

Acting under the instructions of the Joint Committee of Congress, a special stand capable of accommodating one thousand, with the necessary seats, extending from the central steps in a northern direction, has been set apart for the exclusive use of the House and Senate. In this connection I beg to suggest that, in accordance with custom, the stand be turned over when completed to the Sergeant-at-Arms of the Senate, who shall have charge of the same and of the issuing of tickets thereto.

Under the instruction of the Joint Committee, of the one thousand souvenir invitations printed, nine hundred and four have been issued to the persons designated by your Joint Committee, leaving ninety-six only at the disposal of the General Committee. A list of the distribution is herewith submitted.

A grand stand will be erected in front of the central portion of the east front to accommodate the President of the United States, the speakers participating in the ceremonies, the Judiciary, the Diplomatic Corps, and other guests invited under direction of your Joint Committee.

Another stand, extending south from the central portion of the building, is in course of construction to accommodate the band and the grand chorus of fifteen hundred. In relation to the approaches to the building on the 18th of September, some arrangement will have to be made to keep the central steps clear, and I suggest that that be left as a matter of accommodation between the Sergeant-at-Arms of the Senate and the Chairman of the General Committee.

As instructed, letters have been drawn up addressed respectively to the President of the Senate and the Speaker of the House, inviting their respective bodies to be present, copies of which are submitted herewith. I also beg to suggest that, as is usual under such circumstances, an order be passed by each House arranging for their participation in the ceremonies.

On the suggestion of Chairman VOORHEES, it was agreed that motions be made in the Senate and House providing that their respective bodies take a recess at 2 p. m. on the 18th of September and attend the celebration, and Mr. VOORHEES requested Senator SHERMAN to make the motion in the Senate and Mr. COGSWELL to make the motion in the House of Representatives.

At the suggestion of Senator VOORHEES, all details relating to the handling of the crowds at the Capitol on the day of the celebration were delegated to the Sergeants-at-Arms of the Senate and House and the Architect of the Capitol.

It was also ordered that the stands for the Senate and House be turned over to the Sergeants-at-Arms of the respective bodies.

H. Mis. 211——7

Congressional Action

/

CAPITOL, 1893, SOUTHEAST VIEW.

Congressional Action

AUTHORIZING THE CELEBRATION

In the House of Representatives, August 11, 1893, the following action was taken:

Mr. W. D. BYNUM, of Indiana. Mr. Speaker, the gentleman from Maryland [Mr. RAYNER] yields to me for a minute to ask unanimous consent for the consideration of a resolution. I will ask to have it read.

The SPEAKER. The gentleman from Indiana, with the consent of the gentleman from Maryland, desires unanimous consent for the consideration of a joint resolution relating to the exercises commemorative of the hundredth anniversary of the laying of the corner stone of the Capitol. The Clerk will read the joint resolution, after which the Chair will ask if there be objection.

The Clerk read the joint resolution.

Mr. BYNUM. Mr. Speaker, I simply desire to say to the House that this resolution entails no expense on the part of the Government. The funds have been raised by private citizens, and they simply desire the permission and cooperation of the Government.

The SPEAKER. Is there objection to the present consideration of the resolution? [After a pause.] The Chair hears none.

The joint resolution was ordered to be engrossed for a third reading; and being engrossed, it was accordingly read the third time, and passed.

In the Senate, August 14, 1893, the subject was considered, as follows:

A message from the House of Representatives, by Mr. T. O. TOWLES, its Chief Clerk, announced that the House had passed a joint resolution (H. Res. 2) providing for the appropriate commemoration of the laying of the corner stone of the Capitol of the United States, September 18, 1793, in which it requested the concurrence of the Senate.

Mr. VOORHEES. I venture to ask that the Senate consider the joint resolution, and that it be put upon its passage now. For that purpose let it be read. I will merely state that it has been carefully considered and unanimously passed by the other House.

By unanimous consent, the joint resolution was read twice, and considered as in Committee of the Whole.

The joint resolution was reported to the Senate without amendment, ordered to a third reading, read the third time, and passed.

The following is the joint resolution as passed by both Houses, it having received Executive approval August 17, 1893:

Joint resolution providing for the appropriate commemoration of the one hundredth anniversary of the laying of the corner stone of the Capitol of the United States, September 18, 1793.

Whereas the one hundredth anniversary of the laying of the corner stone of the United States Capitol by President GEORGE WASHINGTON, September 18, 1793, is an occasion of national interest becoming the cognizance of Congress; and

Whereas a committee of citizens of the United States, of which LAWRENCE GARDNER, of the District of Columbia, has been elected Chairman, have been appointed to make suitable and appropriate arrangements to duly commemorate the important event, and for the maintenance of order and decorum in the proceedings, and for guarding the Capitol and its grounds from injury: Therefore,

Be it resolved by the Senate and House of Representatives of the United States of America in Congress assembled, That the use of the Capitol Grounds for the ceremonies attending the one hundredth anniversary of the laying of the corner stone of the Capitol for and during the 18th of September, 1893, including processions, literary and musical exercises, and the suitable decoration of the grounds, the Capitol building and its approaches, shall be permitted, under such regulations as may be prescribed by the President of the Senate and the Speaker of the House of Representatives, to insure the safety of the building and the grounds from injury.

That a joint committee of fourteen, to consist of seven Senators, to be appointed by the President of the Senate, and seven Representatives, to be appointed by the Speaker of the House of Representatives, be, and is hereby, constituted to take order in the matter of arranging for the ceremonies at the Capitol, to act with a like committee in number to be selected by the said Citizens' Committee.

APPOINTMENT OF THE JOINT COMMITTEE

In the Senate, August 24, 1893, the Joint Committee on the part of the Senate was appointed, as shown by the following extract from the proceedings:

The VICE-PRESIDENT. Under the joint resolution providing for the appropriate commemoration of the one hundredth anniversary of the laying of the corner stone of the Capitol of the United States, September 18, 1793, the Chair appoints as the committee on the part of the Senate the Senator from Indiana (Mr. VOORHEES), the Senator from Ohio (Mr. SHERMAN), the Senator from North Carolina (Mr. RANSOM), the Senator from New Hampshire (Mr. CHANDLER), the Senator from California (Mr. WHITE), the Senator from Washington (Mr. SQUIRE), and the Senator from Kansas (Mr. MARTIN).

In the House of Representatives, August 25, 1893, the following action was taken:

The SPEAKER laid before the House a message from the Senate announcing the appointment by the Vice-President of a committee on the part of the Senate, consisting of Senators VOORHEES, SHERMAN, RANSOM, CHANDLER, WHITE of California, SQUIRE, and MARTIN, under the joint resolution providing for the appropriate commemoration of the one hundredth anniversary of the laying of the corner stone of the Capitol of the United States, September 18, 1793; which was laid on the table.

The SPEAKER announced the appointment of a like committee on the part of the House, in compliance with the joint resolution, consisting of Messrs. BYNUM, WARNER, BLACK of Illinois, HOUK of Ohio, HENDERSON of Iowa, O'NEILL of Pennsylvania, and COGSWELL.

MAKING THE DAY A HOLIDAY, GRANTING USE OF FLAGS, ETC.

In the House of Representatives, September 3, 1893, further action was taken, as follows:

Mr. BYNUM. Mr. Speaker, I ask unanimous consent for the introduction of a couple of resolutions and their present consideration.

The SPEAKER pro tempore. The Clerk will report the resolution, after which the Chair will ask if there be objection to its consideration.

The Clerk read as follows:

A joint resolution (H. Res. 6) to make the 18th day of September, 1893, a holiday within the District of Columbia.

Be it resolved, etc., That there be added to the days by law declared to be holidays within the District of Columbia the 18th day of September, 1893, the same being the one hundredth anniversary of the laying of the corner stone of the Capitol of the United States.

The SPEAKER pro tempore. Is there objection to the present consideration of the resolution? [After a pause.] The Chair hears none.

The joint resolution was ordered to be engrossed for a third reading; and being engrossed, it was accordingly read the third time, and passed.

Mr. BYNUM. I also ask for the consideration of the other resolution.

The SPEAKER pro tempore. The Clerk will report the resolution, after which the Chair will ask if there be objection to its consideration.

The Clerk read as follows:

A joint resolution (H. Res. 7) to permit the use of certain ensigns, flags, and signal numbers to decorate the Capitol and its approaches, 1893.

Be it resolved, etc., That the Secretary of War and the Secretary of the Navy be, and they are hereby, authorized to deliver to the Architect of the Capitol, for the purpose of decorating the Capitol, its approaches, and grand stands to be erected in the Capitol grounds on the occasion of the centennial celebration of the laying of the corner stone of the Capitol, such of the United States ensigns, flags (except battle flags), signal numbers, and other flags as may be spared, the same to be so delivered to said Architect not prior to the 10th day of September, and to be returned by him by the 30th day of September, 1893.

The SPEAKER pro tempore. Is there objection to the present consideration of this resolution? [After a pause.] The Chair hears none.

The joint resolution was ordered to be engrossed for a third reading; and being engrossed, it was accordingly read the third time, and passed.

On motion of Mr. BYNUM. a motion to reconsider the several votes by which the joint resolutions were passed was laid on the table.

These subjects were considered in the Senate September 4, 1893, as follows:

Mr. VOORHEES. I ask that the joint resolutions which have just come from the House of Representatives be laid before the Senate and put on their passage. I will state that the first is a joint resolution passed by the other House, making the 18th of September a holiday in the District of Columbia. It is the centennial of the laying of the corner stone of the Capitol. The other joint resolution authorizes the use of certain flags and ensigns by the Architect of the Capitol on that day. I should be very glad to have the Senate concur with the action of the House of Representatives and let the matter go along. There being no objection, the joint resolution (H. Res. 6) to make the 18th day of September, 1893, a holiday within the District of Columbia was read twice and considered as in Committee of the Whole.

The joint resolution was reported to the Senate without amendment, ordered to a third reading, read the third time, and passed.

The joint resolution (H. Res. 7) to permit the use of certain ensigns, flags, and signal numbers to decorate the Capitol and its approaches,

September 18, 1893, was read twice and considered as in Committee of the Whole.

The joint resolution was reported to the Senate without amendment, ordered to a third reading, read the third time, and passed.

RESOLUTIONS TO ATTEND

In the Senate, September 11, 1893:

The VICE-PRESIDENT laid before the Senate the following letter; which was read:

WASHINGTON, D. C., *September 11, 1893.*

SIR: The General Committee on the Centennial Celebration of the Laying of the Corner Stone of the Capitol has set apart, under the direction of the Joint Committee appointed under the joint resolution of Congress approved August 17, 1893, a special stand with one thousand seats for the exclusive use of the Senate and House of Representatives, September 18, 1893.

It is the desire of the committee that, following the established precedent of such occasions, the Senate attend the ceremonies as an organized body; and in behalf of the committee I beg to request you to extend this invitation to the United States Senate, and that that honorable body may make such order thereon as may be most appropriate.

Very respectfully,

L. GARDNER,
Chairman General Committee.

Hon. ADLAI E. STEVENSON,
Vice-President United States, President of the Senate.

Mr. SHERMAN, from the Joint Select Committee appointed under the joint resolution providing for the appropriate commemoration of the one hundredth anniversary of the laying of the corner stone of the Capitol of the United States, September 18, 1793, reported the following resolution; which was considered by unanimous consent, and agreed to:

Resolved, That the Senate will attend the ceremonies of the one hundredth anniversary of the laying of the corner stone of the Capitol, September 18, 1893, at 2 o'clock p. m.

That a recess be taken at ten minutes before 2 o'clock p. m. of that day, and the Senate, accompanied by its officers, shall proceed to the place assigned, at the east front of the Capitol.

That the Sergeant-at-Arms of the Senate is directed to make the necessary arrangements to carry out this order.

In the House of Representatives, September 12, 1893:

The SPEAKER. The Chair lays before the House the following communication, which the Clerk will report:

WASHINGTON, D. C., *September 11, 1893.*

SIR: The General Committee on the Centennial Celebration of the Laying of the Corner Stone of the Capitol has set apart, under the direction of the Joint

Committee appointed under the joint resolution of Congress approved August 17, 1893, a special stand with one thousand seats for the exclusive use of the Senate and House of Representatives, September 18, 1893.

It is the desire of the committee that, following the established precedent of such occasions, the House of Representatives attend the ceremonies as an organized body; and in behalf of the committee I beg to request you to extend this invitation to the House of Representatives, and that that honorable body may make such order thereon as may be most appropriate.

Very respectfully,

L. GARDNER,
Chairman General Committee.

Hon. CHARLES F. CRISP,
Speaker House of Representatives, United States.

Mr. COGSWELL. I offer the resolution which I send to the Clerk's desk, and ask for its immediate consideration.

The Clerk read as follows:

Resolved, That the House will attend the ceremonies of the one hundredth anniversary of the laying of the corner stone of the Capitol, September 18, 1893, at 2 o'clock p. m.

That a recess be taken at ten minutes before 2 o'clock of that day, and the House, accompanied by its officers, shall proceed to the place assigned, at the east front of the Capitol. That the Sergeant-at-Arms of the House is directed to make the necessary arrangements to carry out this order.

The SPEAKER. Is there objection to the immediate consideration of this resolution?

There was no objection.

The resolution was agreed to.

ATTENDANCE AT THE CELEBRATION

In the Senate, September 18, 1893:

The VICE-PRESIDENT. The Chair will state to the Senator from Oregon that the Chair is compelled, under the resolution of the Senate, to announce that, the hour of ten minutes to 2 having arrived, it becomes the duty of the Chair to lay before the Senate the resolution adopted by the Senate on the 11th instant, which will be read.

The Secretary read as follows:

Resolved, That the Senate will attend the ceremonies of the one hundredth anniversary of the laying of the corner stone of the Capitol, September 18, 1893, at 2 o'clock p. m.

That a recess be taken at ten minutes before 2 o'clock p. m. of that day, and the Senate, accompanied by its officers, shall proceed to the place assigned, at the east front of the Capitol.

That the Sergeant-at-Arms of the Senate is directed to make the necessary arrangements to carry out this order.

The VICE-PRESIDENT. The Sergeant-at-Arms will execute the order of the Senate.

The Senate, headed by the Vice-President and the Secretary, and preceded by the Sergeant at Arms, thereupon proceeded to the east front of the Capitol to participate in the ceremonies commemorative of the one hundredth anniversary of the laying of the corner stone of the Capitol of the United States.

The Senate returned to its Chamber at 5 o'clock and 15 minutes p. m.

In the House of Representatives, September 18, 1893:

The SPEAKER. The Clerk will report the order adopted by the House.

The Clerk read as follows:

Resolved, That the House will attend the ceremonies of the one hundredth anniversary of the laying of the corner stone of the Capitol, September 18, 1893, at 2 o'clock p. m.

That a recess be taken at ten minutes before 2 o'clock of that day, and the House, accompanied by its officers, shall proceed to the place assigned, at the east front of the Capitol. That the Sergeant-at-Arms of the House is directed to make the necessary arrangements to carry out this order.

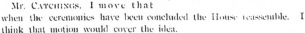

The SPEAKER. The Chair would call the attention of the House to the fact that there is no provision made in this order as to the duration of the recess or the adjournment of the House. Therefore, the Chair would suggest that some motion be made respecting the return to the Hall and the adjournment of the House immediately thereafter.

Mr. CATCHINGS. I move that when the ceremonies have been concluded the House reassemble. I think that motion would cover the idea.

Mr. REED. It is understood that there is to be an adjournment at once on return of the House.

Mr. LIVINGSTON. Why not adjourn now?

The SPEAKER. The only reason why the House can not now adjourn is that the House has agreed to attend this ceremony as a body, and both the House and Senate have agreed to take a recess. However, it can be the understanding, and without objection it will be the understanding, that immediately upon the conclusion of the ceremonies the House will, or such members as return, reassemble, when an adjournment will be had until to-morrow. Without objection that will be the understanding and the order.

There was no objection, and it was so ordered.

The SPEAKER. The House will, in accordance with the order, form in line and proceed to the place of the ceremonies. The officers will accompany the House, and the pages will form in the rear of the members.

Accordingly (at 1 o'clock and 50 minutes), the House, headed by the Speaker and accompanied by its officers, proceeded to the platform prepared for their accommodation in front of the east portico.

The House reassembled at 5 o'clock and 10 minutes.

THE TABLET

In the Senate, April 23, 1894:

The VICE-PRESIDENT laid before the Senate the following communication; which was read:

WASHINGTON, D. C., *April 21, 1894.*

DEAR SIR: The General Committee on the Centennial of the Capitol has donated a bronze tablet, estimated to cost about $900, to be placed upon the exterior southeast wall of the north wing of the original Capitol building, to commemorate the laying of the corner stone of the Capitol, September 18, 1793, by President GEORGE WASHINGTON.

As legislation will be necessary to carry out the purpose of the General Committee, I have the honor to request that the subject may be brought to the attention of Congress, only suggesting that the matter of the inscription upon the tablet be left to the discretion of the Joint Committee appointed under the joint resolution of Congress approved August 17, 1893, and that the selection of the precise locality for the insertion of the tablet, as well as the work connected with such insertion, be placed under the direction of the Architect of the Capitol.

Very respectfully, your most obedient servant,

L. GARDNER,
Chairman General Committee.

HON. ADLAI E. STEVENSON,
President United States Senate.

Mr. VOORHEES. In this connection I ask unanimous consent to introduce and have considered a joint resolution.

The VICE-PRESIDENT. The joint resolution will be read the first time by its title and the second time at length, if there be no objection.

The joint resolution (S. R. 77) providing for the placing of a tablet upon the Capitol to commemorate the laying of the corner stone of the building, September 18, 1793, was read the first time by its title and the second time at length, as follows:

Whereas the General Committee of citizens of the United States, of which LAWRENCE GARDNER is Chairman, have donated to the United States a bronze

Beneath this tablet the corner stone of the
Capitol of the United States of America
was laid by
George Washington
First President September 1793.

On the Hundredth Anniversary
in the year 1893
In presence of the Congress the Executive and the Judiciary
and vast multitudes of the grateful people
of the District of Columbia commemorated the event.

Grover Cleveland	President of the United States.
Adlai Ewing Stevenson	Vice President.
Charles Frederick Crisp	Speaker, House of Representatives.
Daniel Wolsey Voorhees	Chairman Joint Committee of Congress.
Lawrence Gardner	Chairman Citizens Committee.

tablet to be placed upon the Capitol to commemorate the laying of the corner stone of the building, September 18, 1793: Therefore,

Be it resolved by the Senate and House of Representatives of the United States of America in Congress assembled, That the United States accept the said tablet, and that the Architect of the Capitol be, and he is hereby, authorized and directed to cause the same, when approved by the Joint Committee appointed under joint resolution of Congress of August 17, 1893, to be placed in or upon the southeast wall of the north wing of the original Capitol building, upon such suitable place as he, the said Architect, may select, at such distance above the corner stone laid by GEORGE WASHINGTON, September 18, 1793, as in the judgment of said Architect may be best suited to display the same without detracting from the architectural effect of the building.

Mr. VOORHEES. It may not be improper to say that the committee having in charge the centennial celebration of the laying of the corner stone of the Capitol have so well managed their affairs as to have a moderate surplus fund left with which to provide this bronze tablet. The tablet is to be placed at a point to indicate the precise spot where the original corner stone was laid. That locality has been ascertained, and this is a movement to mark the spot for all time to come. I think it a charming and a most excellent thing to do, and the committee which have had charge of this matter are deserving of great credit. They have asked nothing of Congress, they have been at no expense to the Government, and they have the money to spare to make this provision. I thought it best to explain the matter. I ask for the present consideration of the joint resolution.

Mr. GRAY. While the Senator is on his feet in regard to this very appropriate act that has been performed, let me ask him whether the inscription on the tablet is to contain the name of any private person or of the donors of the tablet?

Mr. VOORHEES. I think not.

Mr. GRAY. It ought not to do so.

Mr. VOORHEES. I think it does not, although on that subject I am not at all advised. I should say not, very decidedly. However, that can be easily controlled or managed. I do not think there is any such purpose at all. It is a tablet to mark the precise locality of the original corner stone laid by GEORGE WASHINGTON September 18, 1793.

Mr. GRAY. The good taste of the gentlemen connected with this enterprise would suggest that no such thing should be done; but I think it ought to be assured.

The VICE-PRESIDENT. Is there objection to the present consideration of the joint resolution?

There being no objection, the Senate, as in Committee of the Whole, proceeded to consider the joint resolution.

The joint resolution was reported to the Senate without amendment, ordered to be engrossed for a third reading, read the third time, and passed.

In the House of Representatives, April 24, 1894:

The SPEAKER laid before the House the Senate resolution (S. R. 78) providing for the placing of a tablet upon the Capitol to commemorate the laying of the corner stone of the building, September 18, 1793.

Mr. BYNUM. Mr. Speaker, I ask unanimous consent for the present consideration of the Senate resolution.

The SPEAKER. The gentleman from Indiana asks unanimous consent for the present consideration of the Senate joint resolution, which is before the House for reference. The Clerk will report it, after which the Chair will ask if there be objection.

The resolution was read.

The SPEAKER. Is there objection to the request for the present consideration of the resolution? [After a pause.] The Chair hears none.

The resolution was ordered to a third reading; and it was accordingly read the third time, and passed.

On motion of Mr. BYNUM, a motion to reconsider the vote by which the joint resolution was passed was laid on the table.

PRINTING THE PROCEEDINGS

In the Senate, October 31, 1893:

Mr. VOORHEES, from the Committee on the Library, to whom the subject was referred, reported a bill (S. 1137) to provide for the printing of the report of the Joint Committee of Congress and proceedings at the centennial celebration of the laying of the corner stone of the Capitol; which was read twice by its title, and, on motion of Mr. VOORHEES, referred to the Committee on Printing.

In the Senate, January 16, 1894:

Mr. GORMAN, from the Committee on Printing, reported a joint resolution (S. R. 51) to provide for the printing of the report of the Joint Committee of Congress and proceedings at the centennial celebration of the laying of the corner stone of the Capitol; and submitted a report thereon.

The joint resolution was read the first time by its title.

Mr. GORMAN. I ask for the present consideration of the joint resolution.

By unanimous consent, the joint resolution was read the second time at length, and considered as in Committee of the Whole, as follows:

Resolved by the Senate and House of Representatives of the United States of America in Congress assembled, That the report of the Joint Committee of Congress appointed under the joint resolution approved August 17, 1893, upon the ceremonials at the celebration of the one-hundredth anniversary of the laying of the corner stone of the Capitol of the United States, together with the proceedings and public addresses on the commemoration of that event, be printed in a memorial volume, with such illustrations as may be approved by the Joint Committee on Printing, and that five thousand five hundred copies be printed, fifteen hundred for the use of the Senate, three thousand for the use of the House of Representatives, and one thousand copies for distribution by the Citizens' Committee on the celebration; and the sum of $5,000, or so much thereof as may be necessary, is hereby appropriated, out of any money in the Treasury not otherwise appropriated, to carry this joint resolution into effect.

The joint resolution was reported to the Senate without amendment, ordered to be engrossed for a third reading, read the third time, and passed.

The following is the report (Senate No. 160, second session Fifty-third Congress) made by Mr. GORMAN, from the Committee on Printing:

The Committee on Printing, to whom was referred the bill (S. 1137) "to provide for the printing of the report of the Joint Committee of Congress and proceedings at the centennial celebration of the laying of the corner stone of the Capitol," having considered the same, report it back with the recommendation that it do not pass, and that in lieu thereof the following substitute joint resolution do pass. [Resolution as passed follows.—Ed.]

The provisions of the bill are all retained in the substitute joint resolution with the exception that the distribution of the proposed memorial volume to the House of Representatives is reduced from three thousand five hundred to three thousand. This reduction was found necessary in order to bring the cost of the work within the amount appropriated therefor, and the usual proportion of distribution between the Senate and House of Representatives is still maintained.

The provisions of the bill having relation only to a specific occasion and not embracing any permanent provision of law, a joint resolution has been deemed by the committee the more appropriate method of proceeding.

In the House of Representatives, March 10, 1894:

Mr. RICHARDSON, of Tennessee. Mr. Speaker, I present a privileged report from the Committee on Printing.

The report was read, as follows:

The committee have considered Senate joint resolution No. 51, providing for the printing of the proceedings at the centennial celebration of the laying of the corner stone of the Capitol, and direct me to report the same with the recommendation that it do pass. The estimated cost of the same is about $4,800.

The joint resolution was ordered to a third reading, and it was accordingly read the third time.

The question being taken, on a division the joint resolution was passed—ayes 72, noes 14.

The Capitol

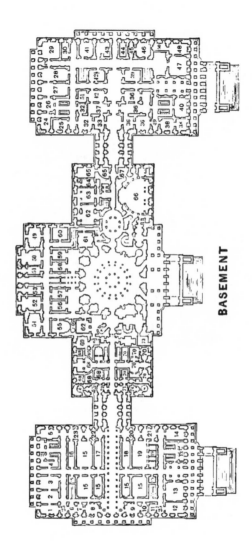

BASEMENT

THE BASEMENT OF THE CAPITOL.

MAIN BUILDING.

Room.
30. Senate Committee on Census.
31. Senate Committee on Manufactures.
31. Senate Committee on Education and Labor.
52. House Committee on Labor.
53. House Merchant Marine and Fisheries.
54. House Coinage, Weights, and Measures.
55. House Committee on Education.
56. House Committee on Revision of the Laws.
57. House Committee on Ventilation and Acoustics.
57. Law Library.
58, 59. Senate Committee on Revolutionary Claims.
60. Storeroom for Library.
61. Storeroom Supreme Court.
62. Senate bathroom.
63. The Supreme Court—Consultation room.
64, 66. Congressional Law Library, formerly the Supreme Court room.
6. Congressional Law Library.
67. Office of Doorkeeper of the House.
68. Office-superintendent of folding room.
69. House Committee on Private Land Claims.
70. Offices of the Chief Clerk of the House.
71. House Committee on Expenditures in the State Department.
72. House Committee on Expenditures in the Interior Department.
73. House Committee on Militia.
74. House Committee on Alcoholic Liquor Traffic.

SENATE COMMITTEES. MALTBY BUILDING.

4. Examine the Branches of Civil service.
19. Relations with Canada.
26. Trespassers on Indian Lands.
29. International Expositions.
38. National Banks.
41. Irrigation and Reclamation of Arid Lands.
41. Corporations organized in the District of Columbia.
43. Geological Survey.
44. Fisheries.
58. Contingent Expenses.
62. Immigration.
71. Transportation and Sale of Meat Products.
73. Five Civilized Tribes of Indians.
New rooms, Forced Reservations.
77. Civil service and Retrenchment.

HOUSE WING.

Room.
1. Committee on Invalid Pensions.
2. Committee on Claims.
3. Committee on Agriculture.
4. Stationery room.
6. Committee on War Claims.
7. Official Stenographers to Committees.
8. Official Reporters of Debates.
9. Committee on the Territories.
10. occupied by the Speaker as a private room.
11. Committee on Library.
12. Committee on Public Buildings and Grounds.
13. House post-office.
13½. Committee on Expenditures in the Post-office Department.
14. Committee on the Post-office and Post-Roads.
15. Clerk's document room.
16. Closet.
17. Box room.
18, 19, 20. Restaurant.
21. Committee on Printing.
22. Committee on Indian Affairs.
22. Committee on Accounts.
23. Committee on Mileage.
24. Committee on Expenditures in the War Department.
25. Elevator.

HOUSE COMMITTEES. TERRACE, SOUTH SIDE.

1, 5. Index room.
2. Committee on Mines and Mining.
3. Committee on Expenditures in the Agricultural Department.
6. Committee on Immigration and Naturalization.
7. Committee on the Election of President and Vice-President and Representatives in Congress.
11. Committee on Irrigation of Arid Lands in the United States.
11. Committee on Expenditures in the Treasury Department.
13. Committee on the Eleventh Census.
15. Committee on Manufactures.

NOTE. Rooms occupied by the House Committee-on-Reform in the Civil Service, Levees and Improvement of Mississippi River, Expenditures in the Department of Justice, Expenditures in the Navy Department, and Expenditures in Public Buildings, are not shown on the diagrams. There are located in the subbasement, west front, on the House side of center of building.

SENATE WING.

Room.
24. Committee on Rules.
25. Committee on The Revision of the Laws.
26. Committee on Patent.
27. Committee on Military Affairs.
27. Committee on Naval Affairs.
29. Committee on the Judiciary.
30. Committee on Pacific Railroads.
32. Committee on Indian Affairs.
33. Stationery room.
34. Restaurant.
36. Stationery room.
37. Committee on Public Lands.
38. Office-superintendent of folding room.
39. Committee on Pensions.
41. Committee on Territories.
42. Ladies' room.
42½. Sergeant-at-Arms' states.
43. Committee on Agriculture.
44. Committee on Enrolled Bills.
56. Committee on Foreign Relations.
57. Senate Post-office.
58. Committee on Post-offices and Post-Roads.
49. Elevator.
40. Gentlemen's room.

SENATE COMMITTEES. TERRACE, NORTH SIDE.

1. To Establish the University of the United States.
2. On organization, Conduct, and Expenditures of Executive Departments.
3. On Indian Depredations.
5. On Transportation Routes to the Seaboard.
4, 6. On the Library.
6. On Coast Defenses.
7. On Railroads.
10. On Immigration.
13. On Improvement of the Mississippi River and its Tributaries.
45, 47. On Mines and Mining.

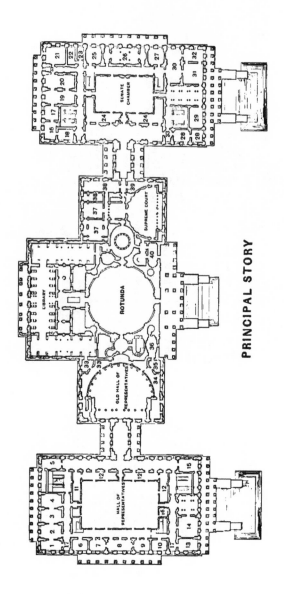

PRINCIPAL STORY

THE PRINCIPAL STORY OF THE CAPITOL.

HOUSE WING.

Room.

1. ⎫ Appropriations
2. ⎭
3. Committee on Rivers and Harbors.
4. Journal, Printing, and File Clerks of the House.
5. Committee on Naval Affairs.
6. Closets.
7. ⎫
8. ⎬ Members' retiring room.
9. ⎭
10. Speaker's room.
11. Hall folding room.
12. Cloakrooms.
13. Office of the Sergeant-at-Arms of the House
14. Committee on Ways and Means.
15. Committee on Military Affairs.
16. House Library.
17. Elevators.

MAIN BUILDING.

Room.

33. House document room.
34. Engrossing and Enrolling Clerks of the House.
35. Committee on Enrolled Bills
36. Office of the Clerk of the House of Representatives. It was in this room, then occupied by the Speaker of the House, that ex-President John Quincy Adams died, two days after he fell at his seat in the House, February 23, 1848.
37. Office of the Clerk of the Supreme Court.
38. Robing room of the Judges of the Supreme Court.
39. Withdrawing room of the Supreme Court.
40. Office of the Marshal of the Supreme Court.

The Supreme Court, formerly the Senate Chamber.

The Old Hall of the House of Representatives is now used as a statuary hall, to which each State has been invited to contribute two statues of its most distinguished citizens.

The Congressional Library contains 590,000 volumes and 150,000 pamphlets.

SENATE WING.

Room.

16. Office of the Secretary of the Senate.
17. Executive Clerk of the Senate.
18. Financial Clerk of the Senate.
19. Chief Clerk of the Senate
20. Engrossing and Enrolling Clerks of the Senate.
21. ⎫ Committee on Appropriations.
22. ⎭
23. Closets.
24. Cloakrooms.
25. Room of the President.
26. The Senators' reception room.
27. The Vice-President's room.
28. Committee on Finance.
29. Official Reporters of Debates.
30. Public reception room
31. Committee on the District of Columbia
32. Office of the Sergeant-at-Arms of the Senate.
33. Elevator.

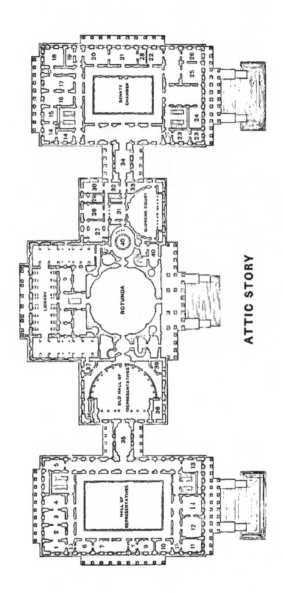

ATTIC STORY

THE ATTIC STORY OF THE CAPITOL.

HOUSE WING.

Room.

1. Committees on Pacific Railroads and Pensions.
2. Committee on Elections.
3. Committee on Banking and Currency.
4. Committee on the District of Columbia.
5. { Committee on Patents.
   { Committee on Railways and Canals.
6. Lobby.
7. Correspondents and journalists' withdrawing room.
8. } Water-closet.
9. }
10. Ladies' retiring room.
11. Committee on the Public Lands.
12. Committee on Commerce.
13. Committee on Foreign Affairs.
14. Committee on the Judiciary.
15. Elevators.

MAIN BUILDING.

Room.

27. Senate Library.
28. Senate Library—Librarian's room.
29. Select Committee on Additional Accommodations for the Library of Congress.
30. Senate Committee on the Construction of the Nicaragua Canal.
31.
32. } Senate document room
33.
34. Superintendent of the Senate documents.
35. House Library.
36.
37. } House document room.
38.
39. Clerk's office.
40. Senate document room.

SENATE WING.

Room.

11. { Committee on Public Building- and Grounds.
    { Committee on Epidemic Diseases.
15. } Committee on Interstate Commerce.
16. }
17. Committee on Privileges and Elections.
18. Committee on Commerce.
19. Committee on Engrossed Bills.
20. Associated Press and United Press, Western Union and Postal Telegraph.
21. Newspaper correspondents' room
22. Ladies' room.
23. Senate and Joint Committee on Public Printing.
24. Conference room of the minority
25. Committee on Claims.
26. Committee on Private Land Claims.
27. Elevator.
28. Correspondents' room.

The Capitol

With Some Notice of Its Architects

[By Edward Clark.]

The original portion of the Capitol is constructed of sandstone from quarries at Aquia Creek, Virginia. Its dimensions are 352 feet 4 inches by 229 feet in depth.

The extensions were begun in 1851, and were occupied by Congress in 1859. The material used is white marble from quarries at Lee, Massachusetts; that in the columns from quarries at Cockeysville, Maryland. The extensions were completed in 1861, the dome in 1863, and the terraces in 1891. The entire frontage of the building is 751 feet 4 inches, and its greatest depth 350 feet. Total cost, including terraces, $14,455,000.

The duty of erecting the public buildings at the permanent seat of government was intrusted by Congress to President WASHINGTON and three Commissioners to be selected by him. In 1792 designs were solicited by this Commission and many plans were presented, but few were thought worthy of consideration. An award was made to Dr. WILLIAM THORNTON and to Mr. STEPHEN HALLETTE for designs by them submitted, and although Dr. THORNTON's plan was followed to some extent, he not being a trained architect, the work of constructing the building was intrusted to STEPHEN HALLETTE.

Mr. HALLETTE came to the United States from France just previous to the Revolution, and established himself at Philadelphia. In 1792 he became Architect of the Capitol, continuing as such until 1794. Upon his retirement the control of the building passed into the hands of JAMES HOBAN, who, as Surveyor of the Public Works, had been previously connected with the construction of the building.

HOBAN was a native of Ireland, and had settled in Charleston, South Carolina, just after the Revolutionary war. His principal work was designing and constructing the President's Mansion. His connection with the Capitol continued for ten years, or until 1802, during which period GEORGE HATFIELD, as architect, was also engaged upon the work, from 1795 to 1798.

HATFIELD was an Englishman by birth, educated as an architect in London. He designed also the old State, War, and Navy Department buildings and the present City Hall.

In 1803 BENJAMIN H. LATROBE was appointed by President

JEFFERSON. He continued in the service until 1817, with the exception of the period of the last war with Great Britain. He restored the portions of the building destroyed during that war.

Mr. LATROBE was born and educated in his profession in England, coming to America in 1796. While living in Philadelphia he designed and constructed many public buildings in that city. It is to his genius we owe the design and finish of the Senate Chamber, now occupied by the Supreme Court, the old Hall of Representatives, and the interior of the wings of the central building. Upon his resignation, in 1817, CHARLES BULL-FINCH, of Boston, Massachusetts, was appointed his successor.

Mr. BULLFINCH constructed the Rotunda, Library rooms, and central porticoes. His connection with the building ceased upon its completion, in 1830, and the Capitol was then placed in charge of the Commissioner of Public Buildings and Grounds until 1851, when the plans of THOMAS U. WALTER for the extension were adopted and he was appointed architect to construct the wings. The work was commenced by laying the corner stone of the south wing July 4, 1851. The entire work was prosecuted with vigor. The Hall of Representatives, south wing, was occupied December 16, 1857, and the Senate Chamber, in the north wing, January 4, 1859.

Mr. WALTER was born in Philadelphia, and had designed many of the principal structures in that city, among which is Girard College for Orphans. He resigned his charge in 1865, and was succeeded by the present Architect, EDWARD CLARK, his pupil, who is a native of the same city.

During Mr. CLARK'S term of service the porticoes of the wings were finished, the marble terraces and grand stairways constructed, and the Capitol grounds extended and remodeled, the latter under plans furnished by FREDERICK LAW OLMSTED, landscape architect.

Among those who have been connected with the construction of the wings of the Capitol and the new dome, the important services of General M. C. MEIGS should be noticed. As captain of Engineers, United States Army, he served for several years in charge of the engineering part of the work, and much is due to his skill in the construction of the dome and in planning and arranging the heating and ventilating apparatus of the wings.

[Added by the Editor.]

Mr. EDWARD CLARK, the present Architect of the Capitol, was appointed in 1865, and is a native of Philadelphia, Pennsylvania. Both his father and brother were expert draftsmen and builders, the former also a teacher of architecture and drawing. Mr. CLARK had an early apprenticeship in drafting and in building mechanics. He entered the office of Mr. THOMAS U. WALTER, then the principal architect in Philadelphia, and soon engaged in work upon competitive plans for the extension of the United States Capitol. Upon the acceptance of these plans and the appointment of Mr. WALTER as Architect of the Capitol, Mr. CLARK accompanied him to Washington as his assistant. In the summer of 1851 he was appointed assistant superintendent of work upon the Patent Office building, under Mr. WALTER, and later served in the same capacity in connection with the construction of the extension of the General Post-Office building, under M. C. MEIGS, captain United States Engineers.

During this service Mr. CLARK was called upon by the Secretary of the Interior, in 1859, to furnish plans for buildings in the Territories. In the Secretary's letter transmitting these plans he was pleased to speak of EDWARD CLARK at that early day as "an experienced architect." In 1865 Mr. CLARK succeeded Mr. WALTER, by appointment from the President, as Architect of the United States Capitol.

For thirty years the growth, development, and care of the Capitol and its surroundings have been his life. He has grown familiar with its every part, its ventilation, water, sewerage, lighting, and heating apparatus, and its avenues, from subbasement to tholus.

The works constructed under his direction will stand as enduring monuments to his ability as an architect and superintendent, being principally—in recapitulation—the completion of the dome, the many-columned porticoes and exterior finish of the Capitol, the construction of the marble terraces, with their grand stairways and approaches, the porticoes and improvements of the Patent Office and the Post-Office buildings, and many other public buildings.

PROCESSION. SEPTEMBER 18, 1793.

The First Corner Stone

The First Corner Stone

Proceedings of September 18, 1793

The following account of the ceremonies of laying the corner stone of the Capitol is copied from the book entitled "The Lodge of Washington: A History of the Alexandria Washington Lodge, No. 22, A. F. and A. M., of Alexandria, Va.," compiled from the original records of the Lodge, by Past Master F. L. BROCKETT, and published in 1876. The quotation credited to "the newspapers of that day" is substantially the report published in the Columbian Mirror and Alexandria Gazette of September 25, 1793. After giving an account of the erection of the southeast corner stone of the District of Columbia, on the 15th of April, 1791, the history above named says:

The next important event of this kind was the laying of the corner stone of the United States Capitol, at the city of Washington, on the 18th day of September, 1793. The Masonic ceremonies were conducted by His Excellency General WASHINGTON, President of the United States, a Past Master of this Lodge, which was present and holding the post of honor. Dr. DICK, elected Worshipful Master in 1789, still in office, invited WASHINGTON to act as Master on this occasion, in accordance with his own wishes and those of the public. The stone was deposited in the southeast corner of the building, instead of the northeast, as is now the custom. The inscription on the plate stated that Alexandria Lodge, No. 22, of Virginia, was present and participated in the ceremonies. The apron and sash worn by WASHINGTON on this occasion were the handiwork of Mrs. General LA FAYETTE, and are now the property of this Lodge.

The following account of the ceremonies was published in the newspapers of that day:

On Wednesday one of the grandest Masonic processions took place, for the purpose of laying the corner stone of the Capitol of the United States, which perhaps was ever exhibited on the like important occasion. About 10 o'clock Lodge No. 9 was visited by that congregation

so graceful to the craft, Lodge No. 22, of Virginia, with all their
officers and regalia; and directly afterwards appeared on the southern
bank of the Grand River Potomack one of the finest companies of volunteer artillery that has been lately seen, parading to receive the
President of the United States, who shortly came in sight with his
suite, to whom the artillery paid their military honors; and His Excellency and suite crossed the Potomack, and was received in Maryland
by the officers and brethren of No. 22, Virginia, and No. 9, Maryland,
whom the President headed, preceded by a band of music, the rear
brought up by the Alexandria Volunteer Artillery, with grand solemnity of march, proceeded to the President's Square, in the city of
Washington, where they were met and saluted by No. 15, of the city
of Washington, in all their elegant badges and clothing, headed by
Brother JOSEPH CLARKE, Right Worshipful Grand Master pro tempore,
and conducted to a large lodge, prepared for the purpose of their reception. After a short space of time, by the vigilance of Brother CLOT-
WORTHY STEPHENSON, Grand Marshal pro tempore, the brotherhood
and other bodies were disposed in a second order of procession, which
took place amid a brilliant crowd of spectators of both sexes, according
to the following arrangement, viz.:

The Surveying Department of the city of Washington
Mayor and Corporation of Georgetown.
Virginia Artillery.
Commissioners of the city of Washington and their attendants.
Stonecutters, mechanics.
The Sword-bearers.
Masons of the first degree.
Bible, etc., on grand cushions.
Deacons, with staffs of office.
Masons of the second degree.
Stewards, with wands.
Masons of the third degree.
Wardens, with truncheons.
Secretaries, with tools of office.
Past Masters, with their regalia.
Treasurers, with their jewels.
Band of music.
Lodge No. 22, of Virginia, disposed in their own order.
Corn, wine, and oil.
Grand Master pro tempore Brother GEORGE WASHINGTON and Worshipful Master
of No. 22, of Virginia.
Grand Sword-bearer.

The procession marched two abreast in the greatest solemn dignity,
with music playing, drums beating, colors flying, and spectators rejoicing, from the President's Square to the Capitol, in the city of Washington, where the Grand Master ordered a halt and directed each file
in the procession to incline two steps, one to the right and one to the
left, and face each other, which formed a hollow oblong square, through

which the Grand Sword-bearer led the van, followed by the Grand Master pro tempore on the left, the President of the United States in the center, and the Worshipful Master of No. 22, Virginia, on the right. All the other orders that composed the procession advanced in the reverse of their order of march from the President's Square to the southeast corner of the Capitol, and the artillery filed off to a destined ground to display their maneuvers and discharge their cannon. The President of the United States, the Grand Master pro tempore, and the Worshipful Master of No. 22, taking their stand to the east of a large stone, and all the craft, forming a circle westward, stood a short time in solemn order. The artillery discharged a volley. The Grand Master delivered the Commissioners a large silver plate with an inscription thereon, which the Commissioners ordered to be read, and was as follows:

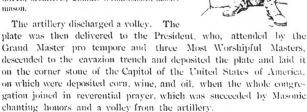

This southeast corner stone of the Capitol of the United States of America, in the city of Washington, was laid on the 18th day of September, 1793, in the thirteenth year of American Independence, in the first year of the second term of the Presidency of GEORGE WASHINGTON, whose virtues in the civil administration of his country have been as conspicuous and beneficial as his military valor and prudence have been useful in establishing her liberties, and in the year of Masonry 5793, by the President of the United States, in concert with the Grand Lodge of Maryland, several lodges under its jurisdiction, and Lodge No. 22, from Alexandria, Va.; THOMAS JOHNSON, DAVID STEUART, and DANIEL CARROLL, Commissioners; JOSEPH CLARK, Right Worshipful Grand Master pro tempore; JAMES HOBAN and STEPHEN HALLETTE, architects; COLLIN WILLIAMSON, master mason.

The artillery discharged a volley. The plate was then delivered to the President, who, attended by the Grand Master pro tempore and three Most Worshipful Masters, descended to the cavazion trench and deposited the plate and laid it on the corner stone of the Capitol of the United States of America, on which were deposited corn, wine, and oil, when the whole congregation joined in reverential prayer, which was succeeded by Masonic chanting honors and a volley from the artillery.

The President of the United States and his attendant brethren ascended from the cavazion to the east of the corner stone, and there the Grand Master pro tempore, elevated on a triple rostrum, delivered an oration fitting the occasion, which was received with brotherly love and commendation. At intervals during the delivery of the oration several volleys were discharged by the artillery. The ceremony ended in prayer, Masonic chanting honors, and a fifteen volley from the artillery.

The whole company retired to an extensive booth, where an ox of 500 pounds' weight was barbecued, of which the company generally partook, with every abundance of other recreation. The festival concluded with fifteen successive volleys from the artillery, whose military discipline and maneuvers merit every commendation. Before dark the whole company departed with joyful hopes of the production of their labor.

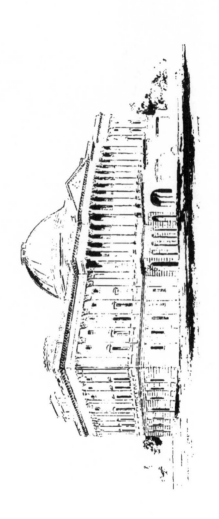

Extension Corner Stone

Extension Corner Stone

The corner stone of the extension of the Capitol was laid by President MILLARD FILLMORE on the 4th day of July, 1851, DANIEL WEBSTER, Secretary of State, delivering the oration. The procession marched from the City Hall down Louisiana avenue to Seventh street, thence to Pennsylvania avenue, thence to the north gate of the Capitol, under the command of RICH-ARD WALLACH, Esq., Marshal of the District of Columbia.

Following is the official programme for the procession and the ceremonies at the Capitol:

THE PROGRAMME

The Marshal of the District of Columbia, to whom has been assigned the duty of making the necessary arrangements for laying the corner stone of the extension of the Capitol, announces the following programme for the occasion:

FIRST DIVISION

J. P. MIDDLETON, Marshal.
Marshal of the District of Columbia and aids.
Military escort.
Officers of the Army and Navy.
Military officers of the several States and Territories.
Officers and soldiers of the Revolution.
Officers and soldiers of the war of 1812.

SECOND DIVISION

Dr. WILLIAM B. MAGRUDER, Marshal.
Civic procession.
Persons present at the laying of the corner stone of the Capitol in 1793.
President of the United States and orator of the day.
Heads of Departments.
Cabinet members of former Administrations.
Committees of Public Buildings of the Senate and House of Representatives.
Architect of the Capitol.
Commissioner of Public Buildings.
Heads of Bureaus.

Judges of the Supreme Court of the United States.
Judges of the United States Courts.
Judges of State Courts.
Diplomatic Corps.
Chaplains of the Thirty-first Congress.
The reverend clergy of the District.
Members of the Senate and House of Representatives.
Governors of States.
Delegations from States and Territories.
Washington Monument Society.
Members of the Smithsonian Institution.
Members of National Institute.
Ex-Mayors of the city of Washington.
The corporate authorities of Alexandria, Georgetown, and Washington.
Members of the Society of the Cincinnati.

THIRD DIVISION

G. A. SCHWARZMAN, Marshal.
The Masonic fraternity.

FOURTH DIVISION

JOSEPH LIBBEY, Marshal.
The several temperance orders and societies.

FIFTH DIVISION

M. THOMPSON, Marshal.
The Washington Benevolent Society.
The German Benevolent Society.
Literary associations, colleges, and schools of the District of Columbia.
Citizens of the several States.
Citizens of Washington.

The military will assemble on Four-and-a-half street, their right resting on D street, opposite the City Hall.

The President of the United States and heads of Departments, members of the judiciary, members of the two Houses of Congress, foreign Ministers, the reverend clergy, and all officers in uniform and on foot are respectfully invited to assemble at the City Hall at 10 o'clock a. m.

The corporate authorities of Baltimore, Alexandria, and Georgetown, and such other corporations as may think proper to participate in the ceremonies of the day, will assemble at the City Hall at 10 o'clock.

The Masonic fraternity will form on Fifth street, with their right resting on D street.

The different temperance societies will take position on E street, with the head of the column resting on Fifth street.

The Washington Benevolent Society, the German Benevolent Society, the literary societies, colleges, and schools will form on Sixth street, their right resting on E street.

The citizens of the States not members of delegations will form on Louisiana avenue, opposite the City Hall.

The procession will move from the City Hall at 11 o'clock precisely, and all bodies intending to join in the procession are requested to be at their respective positions at 10 o'clock a. m.

ROUTE

Down Louisiana avenue to Seventh street; down Seventh street to Pennsylvania avenue, to the north gate of the Capitol.

No carriages will be admitted into the line of procession, and no carriages or horses will be permitted to enter any of the streets or avenues of the route of procession during its progress from the place of assemblage to the Capitol.

The Capitol will be opened for the accommodation of ladies.

ORDER OF CEREMONIES AT THE CAPITOL.

J. MADISON CUTTS, Marshal.

1. Prayer by the Chaplain of the Senate.
2. Laying of the corner stone by the President of the United States.
3. Masonic ceremonies by the Most Worshipful Grand Master and the Grand Lodge of Free Masons of the District of Columbia.
4. Address to the Masonic fraternity by the Grand Master.
5. Address by the Secretary of State.
6. Benediction by the Chaplain of the House of Representatives. Music.

At the conclusion of the ceremonies at the Capitol, a national salute will be fired from a battery at the Capitol, under command of Captain BUCKINGHAM, and at the Navy-Yard, Arsenal, and National Monument.

In the evening there will be a display of fireworks under the direction of THOMAS B. BROWN, pyrotechnist, on the Mall, immediately south of the President's House, where no carriages will be admitted west of Fifteenth street or east of Seventeenth street. The police will see this regulation strictly enforced.

The following gentlemen have been selected as aids to the Marshal of the District of Columbia and assistants to Marshals of Divisions:

AIDS—GEORGE S. GIDEON, WILLIAM H. WINTER.

ASSISTANT MARSHALS—*First Division:* ISAAC HALL, J. D. HOOVER, V. MARION BURCHE, Dr. H. P. HOWARD, J. T. MITCHELL, J. R. ASHBY, RICHARD H. LASKEY, P. H. HOOE, F. LITTLE, G. W. VERBY.

Second Division: JOHN POTTS, THOMAS P. MORGAN, ISAAC R. WILSON, PETER WILSON, WILLIAM R. WOODWARD.

Third Division: GEORGE McNEIR, H. H. HEATH, E. O. PAYNE, R. E. DOYLE, W. O. NILES, JOHN MACAULEY.

Fourth Division: PETER M. PEARSON, LEONIDAS KNOWLES, A. T. HARRINGTON, JOHN D. CLARK, R. GRAY CAMPBELL, J. R. HARBAUGH, JOSEPH LYONS, JOHN C. WINN.

Fifth Division: R. A. MORSELL, ROBERT W. KEYWORTH.

The following-named gentlemen have been selected from States and Territories, and will report to JAMES M. CUTTS for duty as Marshals at the Capitol: SAMUEL B. PARIS, of Maine; GEORGE J. ABBOTT, of New Hampshire; J. H. ADAMS, of Massachusetts; WILLIAM HUNTER, of Rhode Island; A. R. WADSWORTH, of Connecticut; HENRY E. ROBINSON, of Vermont; ARCHIBALD CAMPBELL, of New York; A. VAN WICK, of New Jersey; ROBERT MORRIS, of Pennsylvania; GEORGE P. FISHER, of Delaware; ABRAM BARNES, of Maryland; ROBERT CHEW, of Virginia; WILLIAM W. MORRISON, of North Carolina; HENRY J. KERSHAW, of South Carolina; L. McINTOSH, of Georgia; CHARLES K. SHERMAN, of Alabama; LEWIS L. TAYLOR, of Mississippi; STEPHEN DUNCAN, of Louisiana; GEORGE W. THOMPSON, of Ohio; RICHARD HENRY LEE, of Kentucky; MOREAU BREWER, of

Tennessee; ROBERT G. HEDRICK, of Indiana; NICHOLAS VEDDER, of Illinois; EDWARD M. CLARK, of Missouri; E. B. CULVER, of Arkansas; S. YORKE AT LEE, of Michigan; ROBERT A. LACEY, of Florida; JOSEPH F. LEWIS, of Texas; HENRY CLAY HENDERSON, of Iowa; O. ALEXANDER, of Wisconsin; G. S. OLDFIELD, Jr., of California; A. M. MITCHELL, of Minnesota.

RICHARD WALLACH,
Marshal of the District of Columbia.

THE PROCESSION

The following account of the procession and the ceremonies is condensed from the National Intelligencer of Monday, July 7, 1851, and from other sources:

The national anniversary, which was celebrated on Friday last, was in its important incidents, the fineness of the weather, and its freedom from all untoward circumstances, perhaps the most inter-esting and agreeable ever enjoyed in this metropolis.

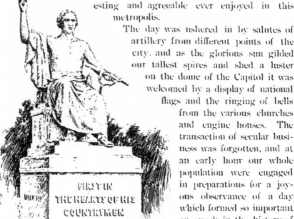

The day was ushered in by salutes of artillery from different points of the city, and as the glorious sun gilded our tallest spires and shed a luster on the dome of the Capitol it was welcomed by a display of national flags and the ringing of bells from the various churches and engine houses. The transaction of secular busi-ness was forgotten, and at an early hour our whole population were engaged in preparations for a joy-ous observance of a day which formed so important an epoch in the history of our country and the world.

In the large Council Chamber of the City Hall were assembled the President of the United States, the members of the Cabinet, officers of the Army and Navy in full uniform, the Mayor and members of the corporation, and various civic bodies.

At the appointed hour the various bodies were drawn into line. The First Division was preceded by the Marshal of the District of Colum-bia, RICHARD WALLACH, Esq., and his aids. The military escort consisted of the Mechanical Artillerists, Captain DUFFY, of Alexandria;

Washington Light Infantry, Captain TATE; National Blues Captain CHESNEY, from Baltimore; National Grays, Captain PETER BACON; Walker Sharpshooters, Lieutenant BIRKHEAD, and Columbian Riflemen, Major McALLISTER, from Baltimore. The visiting companies from Baltimore, though few in number, attracted considerable attention. The battalion was under command of General JOHN MASON, aided by Majors KEYWORTH and RILEY and Captain TATE, of the Infantry.

The array of officers of the Army and Navy was one of the most imposing features of the pageant, including among them thirty or forty brave veterans, many of whom had faithfully spent the flower of their lives in the service of their country, with the Commander in Chief, SCOTT, at the head of the Military Division, and Commodore MORRIS at the head of the Naval, all in full uniform.

In about thirty minutes the procession entered the north gate of the Capitol grounds, and were drawn up in order around the excavation for the corner stone.

CEREMONIES AT THE CAPITOL

After a salutatory by the Marine Band and order being proclaimed, the Rev. M. C. BUTLER, D. D., Rector of Trinity Church and Chaplain of the Senate, opened the ceremonies with the invocation, as follows:

THE INVOCATION

Almighty and immortal God, King of kings and Lord of lords, our Creator, Redeemer, and beautiful Benefactor, we bow before Thee in adoration, thanksgiving, prayer, and praise. Thou hast given us life; Thou hast sent Thy son Jesus Christ to save us from sin and death; Thou hast surrounded us with the means of grace and set before us the hopes of glory. Make us, we beseech Thee, partakers of Thy pardoning love. Give us grace thankfully to accept Thy mercy and earnestly to do Thy will.

We bless Thee, Heavenly Father, for all Thy mercies to us as a nation. Thou art a strong tower to those who fear Thy name. Our fathers trusted in Thee and were delivered. They have declared unto us the noble works which Thou didst in their days and in the old time before them. Thou didst plant them in a goodly heritage; Thou didst unite them in their hour of peril; Thou didst cover their heads and crown them with victory in the day of battle; Thou hast carried us, their children, forward to this happy day in fraternal union, and prosperity, and peace. We beseech Thee to continue these Thy blessings to us and to the generations that shall come after us. Let Thy blessings rest on our beloved Chief Magistrate, the President of the United States; give to our lawgivers wisdom to devise and fidelity to execute such measures as shall promote the public virtue, harmony, and weal. Bless our governors, legislatures, judges, military and naval officers, and all who discharge public trusts. Grant that all estates of men throughout our land, in their several vocations and ministries, may do Thy will and win Thy blessing, that peace and happiness, truth and justice, religion and piety may be established among us for all generations.

We thank Thee, Heavenly Father, for this day, for the mercies which it brings. We bless Thee that Thou didst prosper the purposes and answer the prayers of our fathers, who on this day declared themselves and their country free. We thank Thee for our broad land, our just Constitution, our good laws, our regulated freedom, our Union, our prosperity, and our peace. We thank Thee that we are permitted on this auspicious day to lay the corner stone of an extended Capitol to meet the wants of an enlarged land. Prosper Thou the work of our hands upon us, O Lord our God! Grant that as we lengthen our cords we may strengthen our stakes. Let our liberty ever be guided by law, our knowledge by religion, our power by justice, by mercy, and by peace. May we never use our freedom as a cloak of maliciousness or licentiousness, but remember always that "where the spirit of the Lord is there is liberty." Preserve the States of this Confederacy in perpetual union. Let not the spirit of pride, or of false zeal, or of wicked mischief, unbind or break the bonds which make them one. Let the corner stone of this Capitol and the corner stone of the Union of these States both rest stable and strong until they shall be shaken and broken by the throes of the resurrection morn! O God, our God and our fathers' God, we entreat Thee by Thy multiplied mercies to us in the past, by the momentous interests of the present, by all our fond hopes of future good for ourselves, our children, our country, and the world, we entreat Thee to preserve the States of this Union forever free and forever one! Smile, Heavenly Father, upon the exercises of this day in this place and over all our beloved land. Preserve and bless those who are engaged in them. May hallowed and happy influences attend the celebration of this anniversary more and more from age to age. Graciously accept our services and prayer, and freely pardon all our personal and national transgressions, for the sake of Jesus Christ our Savior. *Amen.*

THOMAS U. WALTER, architect of the new building, then took a survey of the stone and deposited therein a glass jar, hermetically sealed, which contained a variety of valuable historical parchments, coins of the United States, a special paper prepared by the Secretary of State (particularly described by Mr. WEBSTER in his oration), the newspapers of the day, a copy of the oration to be delivered by the Secretary of State, and other memorials.

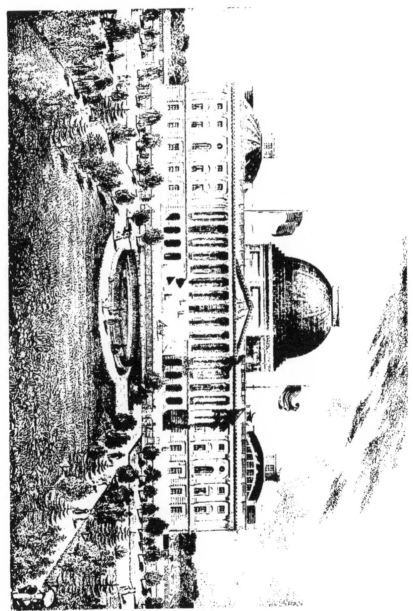

CAPITOL, 1850, EAST FRONT.

(From an old lithograph.)

CORNER STONE LAID

The corner stone of the extension was then, with great dignity and solemnity, laid by MILLARD FILLMORE, President of the United States, after which he gave place to the Masonic fraternity, whose special services were opened with prayer by their Grand Chaplain, Rev. CHARLES A. DAVIS. The "corn of nourishment, the wine of refreshment, and the oil of joy" were severally deposited according to the ritual and practice of the fraternity. The Grand Master examined the stone, applied the square, level, and plumb, and pronounced it properly formed and of suitable material for the purpose for which it was intended. He then placed upon it the corn, wine, and oil, saying as he did so:

May the all-bountiful Creator bless the people of this nation, grant to them all the necessaries, conveniences, and comforts of life; assist in the erection and completion of this edifice, preserve

the workmen from any accident, and bestow upon us all the corn of nourishment, the wine of refreshment, and the oil of joy.

Taking in hand the gavel, the Grand Master, continuing, said:

With this gavel, which was used by the immortal WASHINGTON at the laying of the corner stone of that Capitol, and clothed with the same apron he then wore, I now pronounce this corner stone of this extension of that Capitol well laid, true, and trusty.

Accompanying the last words with three blows of the gavel, the Grand Master then turned to THOMAS U. WALTER, the architect of the extension, and presenting him with the working tools, the square, level, and plumb, he said:

Mr. Architect, I now with pleasure present to you these working tools of your own profession, the square, the level, and the plumb. We, as speculative Masons, use them symbolically; you, as an accomplished architect, well know their use practically, and may the noble edifice here to be erected under your charge arise in its beautiful proportions to completion in conformity with all your wishes, and may your life and health be long continued, and may you see the work go on and the capstone laid under circumstances as auspicious and as happy as those under which this corner stone is this day laid.

ADDRESS OF B. B. FRENCH

The line of procession and the multitude of people now changed position nearer to the front of the stand, the President, his escort, the marshals of the day, and distinguished guests taking their seats upon the lofty platform.

Mr. B. B. French, Grand Master of Masons, then came to the front of the stand and spoke as follows:

My Masonic Brethren: I rise to address you on this occasion deeply impressed with the circumstances which surround me.

Standing as I do in the presence of some of the most exalted men of this nation, and to be followed as I am to be by one admitted by all as emphatically *the orator* of his time, and of whom I can truly say, "He it is, who coming after me is preferred before me, whose shoe's latchet I am not worthy to unloose," you will believe me guilty of no affectation when I say I feel a diffidence which is to me unusual.

Still, as your Grand Master I have a duty to perform, and I shrink from no duty under any circumstances. As has been the custom of our revered order on such occasions, I shall proceed briefly to address you.

I am unable to conceive of a more interesting occasion than this upon which we are here assembled on this anniversary of the birthday of American freedom.

Here we are—the proud dome of our own Capitol towering above us—assembled together from the North and the South, from the East and the West, to perform a duty indicative in itself of the growth and prosperity of this mighty nation.

On the 18th day of September, 1793, was laid, by George Washington, President of the United States and Grand Master of Masons, at least on that occasion, the corner stone of the magnificent edifice before us.

It was doubtless supposed that, when completed according to the plan then adopted, it would be of ample dimensions to accommodate all the wants of the people by whom it was to be erected for ages then to come.

Fifty-eight years have elapsed, and in that comparatively brief space in the ages of Governments we are called upon to assemble here and lay the corner stone of an additional edifice, which shall hereafter tower up, resting firmly on the strong foundation this day planted, adding beauty and magnitude to the people's house, and illustrating to the world the firm foundation in the people's hearts of the principles of freedom and the rapid growth of those principles on this Western Continent.

Yes, my brethren, standing here where fifty-eight years ago Washington stood, clothed in the same Masonic regalia that he then wore, using the identical gavel that he used, we have assisted in laying the foundation of a new Capitol of these United States this day, as Solomon of old laid the foundation of the temple of the living God. "Now, therefore," says the historian Josephus, "the king laid the foundation of the temple very deep in the ground, and the materials were strong stones, and such as would resist the force of time;" and we, following this sublime example, have laid here, deep in the ground, and of strong stones that we trust will resist the force of time, the foundations of a house wherein we hope for lengthened years the representatives of a mighty people shall legislate for the glory, the happiness, and the good of that people.

When the corner stone of the edifice before us was laid in 1793 the Government was justly considered an experiment, and the prediction was again and again made by those who, thank God, turned out to be false prophets, that it would fail. "The wish was" doubtless "father to the thought." But it did not fail! The first census of the United States, in 1791, exhibited a population of less than four millions of souls; at the time of the laying of that corner stone there were probably something over four millions; and now, in less than sixty years, the number has increased to upward of twenty millions! The predictions of failure by the false prophets have themselves utterly failed, while the prayer has been answered and the prophecy fulfilled which WASHINGTON made on assuming the duties of President on the 30th of April, 1789. He then offered up his "fervent supplications to that Almighty Being who rules over the universe, who presides in the councils of nations, and whose providential aid can supply every human defect, that His benediction would consecrate to the liberties and happiness of the people of the United States a government instituted by themselves for these essential purposes; and would enable every instrument employed in its administration to execute with success the functions allotted to his charge."

The ear of the Almighty was opened to that prayer; it was recorded in heaven; and from WASHINGTON down to the present President of the United States, who so worthily and with so much dignity and honor fills the proud station that WASHINGTON filled, it has been answered, and every instrument employed in the administration of this Government has executed with success the functions allotted to his charge.

After this supplication to the Most High, WASHINGTON expressed his conviction that "the foundations of our national policy will be laid in the pure and immutable principles of private morality and the preeminence of a free government be exemplified by all the attributes which can win the affections of its citizens and command the respect of the world." "I dwell," said he, "on this prospect with every satisfaction which an ardent love of my country can inspire, since there is no truth more thoroughly established than that there exists in the economy and course of nature an indissoluble union between virtue and happiness, between duty and advantage, between the genuine maxims of an honest and magnanimous policy and the solid rewards of public prosperity and felicity; since we ought to be no less persuaded that the propitious smiles of Heaven can never be expected on a nation that disregards the eternal rules of order and right which Heaven itself has ordained; and since the preservation of the sacred fire of liberty and the destiny of the republican model of government are justly considered as *deeply*, perhaps as *finally*, staked on the experiment intrusted to the hands of the American people."

This prophecy has been fulfilled. The foundations of our national policy *were* laid in the pure and immutable principles of private morality, and the eternal rules of order and right *having been regarded*, the propitious smiles of Heaven have beamed upon the American people, to whose hands the "experiment" was intrusted. Prophecy has become fact, hope has become fruition, and the experiment on which the destiny of our republican model of government was *deeply* and *finally* staked has been entirely successful.

But, my brethren, we must for a moment reverse this bright picture of the past. As in the fabled mirror, when, under the power of the magic wand, clouds obscure the view for a time, and darkness and desolation shut from the beholder's eye some scene of happiness and joy, so, within a short time past, has there been hovering over the brightness of our political horizon the dark and dismal clouds of disunion, and the time was, and that recently, "when the boldest held his breath" in anticipation of the shock which was expected to overwhelm the Republic.

Thanks to Almighty God, the good old Ship of State weathered the dangers that seemed about to overwhelm her, and, like that glorious old battle ship, the *Constitution*, she has escaped the imminent dangers of a "lee shore," and is again, we hope and trust, in smooth water, with a cloudless horizon all around her. Heaven works not on earth without human means, and men and patriots were inspired in our day of danger to cast themselves resolutely into the breach and strike boldly for the Union. The names of CLAY, WEBSTER, CASS, FOOTE, COBB, DICKINSON, HOUSTON, DOUGLAS, and a host of others, shall live in the history of the dark storm through which we have just passed as the saviors of this glorious galaxy of American States; their names shall stand in history as the pillars of their country in the hour of her darkest trial.

I know I shall be excused for saying that all save one of those whose names I

have mentioned are "brethren of the mystic tie." He to whose eloquence you are about to listen is, if I mistake not, the exception.

To these great, good, patriotic men, aided as they have been by the Executive of the nation, in whose every act a determination not to be misunderstood has been manifested to preserve the Union, do we, as I firmly believe, under God, owe the existence this day of these United States of America. Thanks be to God; thanks to them!

And now, my brethren, do we see nothing here in these ceremonies on this occasion to cheer us? Cold indeed must be our hearts if they can beat on in their regular pulsations, while our eyes behold nothing but a plain rock of granite, hewed and squared, and our ears hear nothing further than "it is a corner stone."

I see in these ceremonies, as it were, the spirit of WASHINGTON among us, renewing the hopes and wishes and prayers that he never failed to offer in his lifetime for the perpetuation of this Union. In that corner stone I perceive the seal set to a renewed lease of the existence of this Union. *Lease*, did I say? No; a deed of warrant in fee simple, to have and to hold to us and our heirs and representatives FOREVER.

In the erection of this new Capitol, adjoining the old one, I see Texas and California and New Mexico come in and unite themselves to our old Union and become one and the same with it; and in leaving this old Capitol untouched I see the old Union, South Carolina and all, standing firmly, proudly, in its glorious strength, unbroken and unbreakable; and let us firmly hope and pray so may it stand FOREVER AND FOREVER.

DANIEL WEBSTER'S ORATION

DANIEL WEBSTER, Secretary of State and orator of the day, then rose from a chair next to President FILLMORE and came to the front of the stand. He was welcomed by the hearty cheers of the multitude and proceeded to read the address which he had prepared, a copy of which had been deposited in the corner stone. He did not, however, confine himself to the manuscript, but occasionally extemporized new thoughts and highly interesting reflections, which, together with the reading, occupied him nearly two hours.

Mr. WEBSTER spoke as follows:

FELLOW-CITIZENS: I congratulate you, I give you joy, on the return of this anniversary; and I felicitate you also on the more particular purpose of which this ever-memorable day has been chosen to witness the fulfillment. Hail! All hail! I see before and around me a mass of faces glowing with cheerfulness and patriotic pride. I see thousands of eyes, turned toward other eyes, all sparkling with gratification and delight. This is the New World! This is America! And this is Washington, the capital of the United States! And where else, among the nations, can the seat of government be surrounded, on any day of any year, by those who have more reason to rejoice in the blessings which they possess? Nowhere, fellow-citizens; assuredly, nowhere. Let us, then, meet this rising sun with joy and thanksgiving.

This is that day of the year which announced to mankind the great fact of American Independence. This fresh and brilliant morning blesses our vision with another beholding of the birthday of our nation; and we see that nation, of recent origin, now among the most considerable and powerful, and spreading over the continent from sea to sea.

Among the first colonists from Europe to this part of America there were some, doubtless, who contemplated the distant consequences of their undertaking and who saw a great futurity; but in general their hopes were limited to the enjoyment of a safe asylum from tyranny, religious and civil, and to respectable subsistence by industry and toil. A thick veil hid our times from their view. But the progress of America, however slow, could not but at length awaken genius and attract the attention of mankind.

In the early part of the next century, Bishop BERKELEY, who, it will be remembered, had resided for some time in Newport, in Rhode Island, wrote his well-known "Verses on the Prospect of Planting ARTS and LEARNING in AMERICA." The last stanza of this little poem seems to have been produced by a high poetical inspiration:

> Westward the course of empire takes its way;
> The first four acts already past,
> A fifth shall close the drama with the day;
> Time's noblest offspring is the last.

This extraordinary prophecy may be considered only as the result of long foresight and uncommon sagacity; of a foresight and sagacity stimulated, nevertheless, by excited feeling and high enthusiasm. So clear a vision of what America would become was not founded on square miles, or on existing numbers, or on any vulgar laws of statistics. It was an intuitive glance into futurity; it was a grand conception, strong, ardent, glowing, embracing all time since the creation of the world and all regions of which that world is composed, and

judging the future by just analogy with the past. And the inimitable imagery
and beauty with which the thought is expressed, joined to the conception itself,
render it one of the most striking passages in our language.

On the day of the Declaration of Independence our illustrious fathers performed
the first act of this drama, an act in real importance infinitely exceeding that
for which the great English poet invoked

> A muse of fire. * * *
> A kingdom for a stage, princes to act,
> And monarchs to behold the swelling scene!

The muse inspiring our fathers was the Genius of Liberty, all on fire with a
sense of oppression and a resolution to throw it off; the whole world was the
stage, and higher characters than princes trod it; and instead of monarchs,
countries and nations and the age beheld the swelling scene. How well the
characters were cast, and how well each acted his part, and what emotions the
whole performance excited, let history now and hereafter tell.

At a subsequent period, but before the Declaration of Independence, the Bishop
of St. Asaph published a discourse in which the following remarkable passages
are found:

> It is difficult for man to look into the destiny of future ages. The designs of Providence are
> too vast and complicated and our own powers are too narrow to admit of much satisfaction to
> our curiosity. But when we see many great and powerful causes constantly at work, we can
> not doubt of their producing proportionable effects.
>
> The Colonies of North America have not only taken root and acquired strength, *but seem has-
> tening with an accelerated progress to such a powerful state as may introduce a new and important
> change in human affairs.*
>
> Descended from ancestors of the most improved and enlightened part of the Old World, they
> receive, as it were by inheritance, all the improvements and discoveries of their mother country;
> and it happens, fortunately for them, to commence their flourishing state at a time when the
> human understanding has attained to the free use of its powers and learned to act with vigor
> and certainty. They may avail themselves not only of the experience and industry but even of
> the errors and mistakes of our former days. Let it be considered for how many ages a great
> part of the world appears not to have thought at all; how many more they have been busied in
> forming systems and conjectures, while reason has been lost in a labyrinth of words, and they
> never seem to have suspected on what frivolous matters their minds were employed.
>
> And let it be well understood, what important discoveries have been
> made in a few years by a few countries, with our own at their head, which have at last discov-
> ered the right method of using their faculties.
>
> May we not reasonably expect that a number of provinces, possessed of those advantages, and
> quickened by mutual emulation, with only the common progress of the human mind, should very
> considerably enlarge the boundaries of science?
>
> The vast continent itself, over which they are gradually spreading, may be considered as a
> treasure, yet untouched, of natural productions that shall hereafter afford ample matter for
> commerce and contemplation. And if we reflect what a stock of knowledge may be accumulated
> by the constant progress of industry and observation, fed with fresh supplies from the stores
> of nature, assisted sometimes by those happy strokes of chance which mock all the powers of
> invention, and sometimes by those superior characters which arise occasionally to instruct and
> enlighten the world, it is difficult even to imagine to what height of improvement their discoveries
> may extend.
>
> *And perhaps they may make as considerable advances in the arts of civil government and the
> conduct of life.* We have reason to be proud, and even jealous, of our excellent constitution; but
> those equitable principles upon which it was formed, an equal representation (the best discovery
> of political wisdom), and a just and commodious distribution of power, which with us were the
> price of civil wars and the rewards of the virtues and sufferings of our ancestors, descend to them
> as a natural inheritance, without toil or pain.
>
> *But must they rest here, as in the utmost effort of human genius? Can chance and time, the wisdom
> and the experience of public men, suggest no new remedy against the evils which vices and ambition
> are perpetually apt to cause?* May they not hope, without presumption, to preserve a greater
> zeal for piety and public devotion than we have done? For surely it can hardly happen to
> them, as it has to us, that when religion is best understood and rendered most pure and rea-
> sonable, then should be the precise time when many cease to believe and practice it, and all in
> general become most indifferent to it.

May they not possibly be more successful than their mother country in preserving that reverence and authority which is due to the laws? to those who make and to those who execute them? *May not a method be invented of procuring some tolerable share of the comforts of life to those inferior useful ranks of men to whose industry we are indebted for the whole? Time and discipline may discover some means to correct the extreme inequalities of condition between the rich and the poor, so dangerous to the innocence and happiness of both.* They may be fortunately led by habit and choice to despise that luxury which is considered with us the true enjoyment of wealth. They may have little relish for that ceaseless hurry of amusements which is pursued in this country without pleasure, exercise, or enjoyment. And perhaps, after trying some of our follies and caprices and rejecting the rest, they may be led by reason and experiment to that old simplicity which was first pointed out by Nature, and has produced those models which we still admire in arts, eloquence, and manners. *The diversity of new scenes and situations which so many growing States must necessarily pass through may introduce changes in the fluctuating opinions and manners of men which we can form no conception of; and not only the gracious disposition* of Providence, but the visible preparation of causes, seems to indicate strong tendencies toward a general improvement.

Fellow-citizens, this gracious dispensation of Providence and this visible preparation of causes at length brought on the hour for decisive action. On the 4th of July, 1776, the representatives of the United States of America in Congress assembled declared that these United Colonies are, and of right ought to be, FREE AND INDEPENDENT STATES.

This declaration, made by most patriotic and resolute men, trusting in the justice of their cause and the protection of Heaven, and yet made not without deep solicitude and anxiety, has now stood for seventy-five years and still stands. It was sealed in blood. It has met dangers and overcame them; it has had enemies and it has conquered them; it has had detractors and it has abashed them all; it has had doubting friends, but it has cleared all doubts away; and now, to-day, raising its august form higher than the clouds, twenty millions of people contemplate it with hallowed love, and the world beholds it and the consequences which have followed from it with profound admiration.

This anniversary animates and gladdens and unites all American hearts. On other days of the year we may be party men, indulging in controversies more or less important to the public good; we may have likes and dislikes and we may maintain our political differences, often with warm and sometimes with angry feelings. But to-day we are Americans all; and all nothing but Americans. As the great luminary over our heads, dissipating mists and fogs, now cheers the whole hemisphere, so do the associations connected with this day disperse all cloudy and sullen weather, and all noxious exhalations in the minds and feelings of true Americans. Every man's heart swells within him; every man's port and bearing become somewhat more proud and lofty as he remembers that seventy-five years have rolled away and that the great inheritance of liberty is still his; his, undiminished and unimpaired; his in all its original glory; his to enjoy; his to protect; and his to transmit to future generations.

Fellow-citizens, this inheritance which we enjoy to-day is not only an inheritance of liberty, but of our own peculiar American liberty. Liberty has existed in other times, in other countries, and in other forms. There has been a Grecian liberty, bold and powerful, full of spirit, eloquence, and fire, a liberty which produced multitudes of great men and has transmitted one immortal name, the name of DEMOSTHENES, to posterity. But still it was a liberty of disconnected states, sometimes united, indeed, by temporary leagues and confederacies, but often involved in wars between themselves. The sword of Sparta turned its sharpest edge against Athens, enslaved her, and devastated Greece, and, in her turn, Sparta was compelled to bend before the power of Thebes; and let it be ever remembered, especially let the truth sink deep into American minds, that it was the WANT OF UNION among her several states which finally gave the mastery of all Greece to PHILIP of Macedon.

And there has also been a Roman liberty, a proud, ambitious, domineering spirit, professing free and popular principles in Rome itself, but, even in the best days of the republic, ready to carry slavery and chains into her provinces and through every country over which her eagles could be borne. Who ever heard of liberty in Spain, or Gaul, or Germany, or Britain in the days of Rome? There was none such. As the Roman Empire declined, her provinces, not instructed in the principles of free popular government, one after another declined also, and when Rome herself fell in the end, all fell together.

I have said, gentlemen, that our inheritance is an inheritance of American liberty. That liberty is characteristic, peculiar, and altogether our own. Nothing like it existed in former times nor was known in the most enlightened states of antiquity; while with us its principles have become interwoven into the minds of individual men, connected with our daily opinions and our daily habits, until it is, if I may so say, an element of social as well as of political life; and the consequence is, that to whatever region an American citizen carries himself, he takes with him, fully developed in his own understanding and experience, our American principles and opinions, and becomes ready at once, in cooperation with others, to apply them to the formation of new governments. Of this a most wonderful instance may be seen in the history of the State of California.

On a former occasion I have ventured to remark that "it is very difficult to establish a free conservative government for the equal advancement of all the interests of society. What has Germany done; learned Germany, fuller of ancient lore than all the world beside? What has Italy done? What have they done who dwell on the spot where CICERO lived? They have not the power of self-government which a common town meeting with us possesses. Yes, I say that those persons who have gone from our town meetings to dig gold in California are more fit to make a republican government than any body of men in Germany or Italy because they have learned this one great lesson, that there is no security without law, and that under the circumstances in which they are placed, where there is no military authority to cut their throats, there is no sovereign will but the will of the majority; that, therefore, if they remain, they must submit to that will." And this I believe to be strictly true.

Now, fellow-citizens, if your patience will hold out, I will venture, before proceeding to the more appropriate and particular duties of the day, to state in a few words what I take these American political principles to be. They consist, as I think, in the first place, in the establishment of popular governments on the basis of representation, for it is plain that a pure democracy, like that which existed in some of the states of Greece, in which every individual had a direct vote in the enactment of all laws, can not possibly exist in a country of wide extent. This representation is to be made as equal as circumstances will allow. Now, this principle of popular representation prevailing either in all the branches of governments or in some of them, has existed in these States almost from the days of the settlements at Jamestown and Plymouth, borrowed, no doubt, from the example of the popular branch of the British legislature. The representation of the people in the British House of Commons was indeed originally very unequal, and it is yet not equal. Indeed, it may be doubted whether the appearance of knights and burgesses, assembling on the summons of the Crown, was not intended at first as an assistance and support to the royal prerogative in matters of revenue and taxation rather than as a mode of ascertaining popular opinion. Nevertheless, representation had a popular origin and savored more and more of the character of that origin as it acquired by slow degrees greater and greater strength in the actual government of the country. In fact, the constitution of the House of Commons was a form of representation, however unequal; numbers were counted and majorities prevailed. And when our ancestors, acting upon this example, introduced more equality of representation, the idea assumed a more rational and distinct shape. At any rate, this manner of exercising popular power was familiar to our fathers when they settled on this continent. They adopted it, and generation has risen up after generation, all acknowledging it and becoming acquainted with its practice and its forms.

And the next fundamental principle in our system is, that the will of the majority, fairly expressed through the means of representation, shall have the force of law; and it is quite evident in a country without thrones or aristocracies or privileged castes or classes there can be no other foundation for law to stand upon.

And, as the necessary result of this, the third element is, that the law is the supreme rule for the government of all. The great sentiment of ALCÆUS, so beautifully presented to us by Sir WILLIAM JONES, is absolutely indispensable to the construction and maintenance of political systems:

> What constitutes a state?
> Not high-raised battlements or labored mound,
>   Thick wall, or moated gate;
> Not cities proud, with spires and turrets crowned;
>   Not bays and broad-arm'd ports,
> Where, laughing at the storm, rich navies ride;
>   Not starr'd and spangled courts,
> Where low-brow'd baseness wafts perfume to pride.
>   No—MEN, high-minded MEN,
> With powers as far above dull brutes endued
>   In forest, brake, or den,
> As beasts excel cold rock and brambles rude;
>   Men who their duties know,
> But know their rights, and knowing, dare maintain,
>   Prevent the long-aim'd blow,
> And crush the tyrant while they rend the chain.
>   These constitute a state;
> And SOVEREIGN LAW, that state's collected will,
>   O'er thrones and globes elate,
> Sits empress, crowning good, repressing ill.

And, finally, another most important part of the great fabric of American liberty is, that there shall be written constitutions, founded on the immediate authority of the people themselves, and regulating and restraining all the powers conferred upon government, whether legislative, executive, or judicial.

This, fellow-citizens, I suppose to be a just summary of our American principles, and I have on this occasion sought to express them in the plainest and in the fewest words. The summary may not be entirely exact, but I hope it may be sufficiently so to make manifest to the rising generation among ourselves, and to those elsewhere who may choose to inquire into the nature of our political institutions, the general theory upon which they are founded. And I now proceed to add that the strong and deep-settled conviction of all intelligent persons among us is, that in order to support a useful and wise government upon these popular principles the general education of the people and the wide diffusion of pure morality and true religion are indispensable. Individual virtue is a part of public virtue. It is difficult to see how there can remain morality in the Government when it shall cease to exist among the people, or how the aggregate of the political institutions, all the organs of which consist only of men, should be wise and beneficent, and competent to inspire confidence, if the opposite qualities belong to the individuals who constitute those organs and make up that aggregate.

And now, fellow-citizens, I take leave of this part of the duty which I proposed to perform, and once more felicitating you and myself that our eyes have seen the light of this blessed morning, and that our ears have heard the shouts with which joyous thousands welcome its **return**, and joining with you in the hope that every revolving year shall renew these rejoicings to the end of time, I proceed to address you, shortly, upon the particular occasion of our assembling here to-day.

Fellow-citizens, by the act of Congress of the 30th of September, 1850, provision was made for the extension of the Capitol, according to such plan as might be approved by the President of the United States, and the necessary sums to be expended under his direction by such architect as he might appoint. This measure was imperatively demanded for the use of the legislative and judiciary departments, the public libraries, the occasional accommodation of the Chief Executive Magistrate, and for other objects. No act of Congress incurring a large expenditure has received more general approbation of the people. The President has proceeded to execute this law. He has approved a plan; he has appointed an architect; and all things are now ready for the commencement of the work.

The anniversary of National Independence appeared to afford an auspicious occasion for laying the foundation stone of the additional building. That ceremony has now been performed by the President himself in the presence and view of this multitude. He has thought that the day and the occasion made a united and an imperative call for some short address to the people here assembled; and it is at his request that I have appeared before you to perform that part of the duty which was deemed incumbent upon us.

Beneath the stone is deposited, among other things, a list of which will be published, the following brief account of the proceedings of this day, in my handwriting:

On the morning of the first day of the seventy-sixth year of the Independence of the United States of America, in the city of Washington, being the 4th day of July, 1851, this stone, designed as the corner stone of the extension of the Capitol, according to a plan approved by the President, in pursuance of an act of Congress, was laid by MILLARD FILLMORE, President of the United States, assisted by the Grand Master of the Masonic lodges, in the presence of many Members of Congress, of officers of the executive and judiciary departments, National, State, and District, of officers of the Army and Navy, the corporate authorities of this and neighboring cities, many associations, civil and military and Masonic, officers of the Smithsonian Institution and National Institute, professors of colleges and teachers of schools of the District with their students and pupils, and a vast concourse of people from places near and remote, including a few surviving gentlemen who witnessed the laying of the corner stone of the Capitol by President WASHINGTON on the 18th day of September, 1793.

If it shall hereafter be the will of God that this structure shall fall from its base, that its foundation be upturned and this deposit brought to the eyes of men, be it then known that on this day the Union of the United States of America stands firm; that their Constitution still exists unimpaired and with all its original usefulness and glory; growing every day stronger and stronger in the affections of the great body of the American people and attracting more and more the admiration of the world. And all here assembled, whether belonging to public life or to private life, with hearts devoutly thankful to Almighty God for the preservation of the liberty and happiness of the country, unite in sincere and fervent prayers that this deposit and the walls and arches, the domes and towers, the columns and entablatures, now to be erected over it, may endure forever!

GOD SAVE THE UNITED STATES OF AMERICA!

DANIEL WEBSTER,
Secretary of State of the United States.

Fellow-citizens, fifty-eight years ago WASHINGTON stood on this spot to execute a duty like that which has now been performed. He then laid the corner stone of the original Capitol. He was at the head of the Government at that time, weak in resources, burdened with debt, just struggling into political existence and respectability, and agitated by the heaving waves which were overturning European thrones. But even then, in many important respects, the Government was strong. It was strong in WASHINGTON's own great character; it was strong in the wisdom and patriotism of other eminent public men, his political associates and fellow laborers, and it was strong in the affections of the people.

Since that time astonishing changes have been wrought in the condition and prospects of the American people, and a degree of progress witnessed with which the world can furnish no parallel. As we review the course of that progress wonder and amazement arrest our attention at every step. The present occasion, although allowing of no lengthened remarks, may yet perhaps admit of a short comparative statement between important subjects of national interest as they existed at that day and as they now exist. I have adopted for this purpose the tabular form of statement as being the most brief and the most accurate.

Comparative table.

	1793.	1851.
Number of States	15	31
Representatives and Senators in Congress	135	295
Population of the United States	3,929,328	23,367,498
Population of Boston	18,038	136,871
Population of Baltimore	13,503	169,054
Population of Philadelphia	42,520	409,045
Population of New York City	33,131	515,507
Population of Washington	....	40,075
Population of Richmond	4,000	27,582
Population of Charleston	16,359	42,985
Amount of receipts into the Treasury	$5,720,624	$43,774,848
Amount of expenditures of the United States	$7,529,575	$39,355,268
Amount of imports	$31,100,000	$178,138,318
Amount of exports	$26,109,000	$151,898,720
Amount of tonnage	520,764	3,535,454
Area of the United States, in square miles	805,461	3,314,365
Rank and file of the Army	5,120	10,000
Militia (enrolled)	....	2,009,360
Navy of the United States (vessels)	....	76
Navy armament (ordnance)	....	2,012
Treaties and conventions with foreign powers	9	90
Light-houses and light-boats	12	372
Expenditures for light-boats	12,061	529,265
Area of the first Capitol building (square feet)	11,543	....
Area of the present Capitol, including extension (acres)	....	4½
Lines of railroads, in miles	....	8,380
Lines of telegraph, in miles	....	15,000
Number of post-offices	889	21,551
Number of miles of post route	5,642	178,762
Amount of revenue from post-offices	$104,747	$5,502,971
Amount of expenditures of Post-Office Department	$72,090	$5,212,933
Number of miles mail transportation	....	46,541,423
Number of colleges	19	121
Public libraries	35	694
Volumes in libraries	75,053	2,201,632
School libraries	....	10,000
Volumes in libraries	....	2,000,000

In respect to the growth of Western trade and commerce, I extract a few sentences from a very valuable address before the Historical Society of Ohio, by WILLIAM D. GALLAGHER, Esq., 1850:

A few facts will exhibit as well as a volume the wonderful growth of Western trade and commerce. Previous to the year 1800 some eight or ten keel boats of twenty or twenty-five tons each performed all the carrying trade between Cincinnati and Pittsburg. In 1802 the first Government vessel appeared on Lake Erie. In 1811 the first steamboat (the *Orleans*) was launched at Pittsburg. In 1826 the waters of Michigan were first plowed by the keel of a steamboat, a pleasure trip to Green Bay being planned and executed in the summer of this year. In 1832 a steamboat first appeared at Chicago. At the present time the entire number of steamboats running on the Mississippi and Ohio and their tributaries is more probably over than under six hundred, the aggregate tonnage of which is not short of one hundred and forty thousand—a larger number of steamboats than England can claim and a greater steam commercial marine than that employed by Great Britain and her dependencies.

And now, fellow-citizens, having stated to you this infallible proof of the growth and prosperity of the nation, I ask you, and I would ask every man, whether the Government which has been over us has proved itself an infliction or a curse to the country or any part of it?

Ye men of the South, of all the original Southern States, what say you to all this? Are you, or any of you, ashamed of this great work of your fathers? Your fathers were not they who stoned the prophets and killed them. They were among the prophets, they were of the prophets; they were themselves the prophets.

Ye men of Virginia, what do you say to all this? Ye men of the Potomac, dwelling along the shores of that river where WASHINGTON lived, and where he died, and where his remains now rest—ye, so many of whom may see the domes of the Capitol from your own homes—what do you say?

Ye men of James River and the Bay, places consecrated by the early settlement of your Commonwealth, what do you say? Do you desire, from the soil of your State or as you travel to the North, to see these halls vacated, their beauty and ornaments destroyed, and their national usefulness clean gone forever?

Ye men beyond the Blue Ridge, many thousands of whom are nearer to this Capitol than to the seat of government of your own State, what do you think of breaking this great association into fragments of States and of people? I know some of you, and I believe you all would be almost as much shocked at the announcement of such a catastrophe as if you were to be informed that the Blue Ridge itself would soon totter to its base. And ye men of western Virginia, who occupy the great slope from the top of the Alleghany to the Ohio and Kentucky, what course do you propose to yourselves by disunion? If you "secede," what do you "secede" from, and what do you "accede" to? Do you look for the current of the Ohio to change, and to bring you and your commerce to the tide waters of Eastern rivers? What man in his senses can suppose that you will remain part and parcel of Virginia a month after Virginia should have ceased to be part and parcel of the United States?

The secession of Virginia! The secession of Virginia, whether alone or in company, is most improbable, the greatest of improbabilities. Virginia, to her everlasting honor, acted a great part in framing and establishing the present Constitution. She hath had her reward and her distinction. Seven of her noble sons have each filled the Presidency and enjoyed the highest honors of the country. Dolorous complaints come up to us from the South that Virginia will not head the procession of secession and lead the other Southern States out of the Union. This would be something of a marvel, certainly, considering how much pains Virginia took to lead these same States into the Union, and considering, too, that she has partaken as largely of its benefits and its government as any other State.

And ye men of the other Southern States, members of the old thirteen; yes, members of the old thirteen—that touches my regard and my sympathies—North Carolina, Georgia, South Carolina, what page in your history or in the history of any one of you is brighter than those which have been recorded since the Union was formed, or through what effect has your prosperity been greater or your peace and happiness better secured? What names even has South Carolina, now so much dissatisfied—what names has she of which her intelligent sons are more proud than those which have been connected with the government of South Carolina? In Revolutionary times and in the earliest days of the Constitution there was no State more honored or more deserving to be honored. Where is she now? And "What a fall is there, my countrymen!" But I leave her to her own reflections, commending to her with all my heart the due consideration of her own example in times now gone by.

Fellow-citizens, there are some diseases of the mind as well as of the body, diseases of communities as well as diseases of individuals, that must be left to their own cure; at least it is wise to leave them so until the last critical moment shall arrive.

I hope it is not irreverent, and certainly it is not intended as reproach, when I say that I know no stronger expression in our language than that which describes the restoration of a wayward son, "He came to himself." He had broken away from all the ties of love, family, and friendship. He had forsaken everything which he had once regarded in his father's house. He had quitted his natural sympathies, affections, and habits, and taken his journey into a far country. He had gone away from himself and out of himself. But misfortunes overtook him and famine threatened him with starvation and death. No entreaties from home followed him to beckon him back; no admonition from others warned him of his fate. But the hour of reflection had come, and nature and conscience wrought with him until at length "he *came* to himself."

And now, ye men of the new States of the South! You are not of the original thirteen. The battle had been fought and won, the revolution achieved, and the Constitution established before your States had any existence as States. You came into a prepared banquet and had seats assigned you at the table just as honorable as those which were filled by older guests. You have been and are singularly prosperous; and if anyone should deny this you would at once contradict his assertion. You have bought vast quantities of choice and excellent land at the lowest price; and if the public domain has not been lavished upon you, you yourselves will admit that it has been appropriated to your own uses by a very liberal hand. And yet in some of these States—not in all—persons are found in favor of a dissolution of the Union, or of secession from it. Such opinions are expressed even where the general prosperity of the community has been the most rapidly advanced. In the flourishing and interesting State of Mississippi, for example, there is a large party which insists that her grievances are intolerable; that the whole body politic is in a state of suffering, and all along and through her whole extent on the Mississippi a loud cry rings that her only remedy is "Secession!" "Secession!" Now, gentlemen, what infliction does the State of Mississippi suffer under? What oppression prostrates her strength or destroys her happiness? Before we can judge of the proper remedy we must know something of the disease; and for my part I confess that the real evil existing in the case appears to me to be a certain inquietude or uneasiness growing out of a high degree of prosperity and consciousness of wealth and power, which sometimes leads men to be ready for changes and to push on to still higher elevation. If this be the truth of the matter, the doctors are about right. If the complaint spring from overwrought prosperity, for that disease I have no doubt that "secession" would prove a sovereign remedy.

But I return to the leading topic on which I was engaged. In the department of invention there have been wonderful applications of science to arts within the last sixty years. The spacious hall of the Patent Office is at once the repository and proof of American inventive art and genius. Their results are seen in the numerous improvements by which human labor is abridged.

Without going into details, it may be sufficient to say that many of the applications of steam to locomotion and manufactures; of electricity and magnetism to the production of mechanical motion, to the electrical telegraph, to the registration of astronomical phenomena, to the art of multiplying engravings; the introduction and improvement among us of all the important inventions of the Old World, are strikingly indicative of this country in the useful arts.

The network of railroads and telegraph lines by which this vast country is reticulated have not only developed its resources, but united emphatically, in metallic bands, all parts of the Union.

The hydraulic works of New York, Philadelphia, and Boston surpass in extent and importance those of ancient Rome.

But we have not confined our attention to the immediate application of science to the useful arts. We have entered the field of original research and have enlarged the bounds of scientific knowledge.

Sixty years ago, besides the brilliant discoveries of Franklin in electricity scarcely anything had been done among us in the way of original discovery. Our men of science were content with repeating the experiments and diffusing a knowledge of the discoveries of the learned of the Old World without attempting to add a single new fact or principle to the existing stock. Within the last twenty-five or thirty years a remarkable improvement has taken place in this respect. Our natural history has been explored in all its branches; our geology has been investigated with results of the highest interest to practical and theoretical science; discoveries have been made in pure chemistry and electricity which have received the approbation of the world. The advance which has been made in meteorology in this country within the last twenty years is equal to that made during the same period in all the world besides.

In 1793 there was not in the United States an instrument with which a good observation of the heavenly bodies could be made. There are now instruments at Washington, Cambridge, and Cincinnati equal to those at the best European observatories; and the original discoveries in astronomy within the last five years in this country are among the most brilliant of the age. I can hardly refrain from saying in this connection that LA PLACE has been translated, explained, and in some instances his illustrations improved by BOWDITCH.

Our knowledge of the geography and topography of the American continent has been rapidly extended by the labor and science of the officers of the United States Army, and discoveries of much interest on distant seas have resulted from the enterprise of the Navy.

In 1807 a survey of the coast of the United States was commenced, which at that time it was supposed no American was competent to direct. The work has, however, grown within the last few years, under a native superintendent, in importance and extent beyond any enterprise of the kind ever before attempted.

These facts conclusively prove that a great advance has been made among us, not only in the application of science to the wants of ordinary life, but to science itself in its highest branches—in its application to satisfy the cravings of the immortal mind.

In respect to literature, with the exception of some books of elementary education, and some theological treatises, of which scarcely any but those of JONATHAN EDWARDS have any permanent value, and some works on local history and politics, like HUTCHINSON'S Massachusetts, JEFFERSON'S Notes on Virginia, the Federalist, BELKNAP'S New Hampshire, and MORSE'S Geography, and a few others, America had not produced a single work of any repute in literature. We were almost wholly dependent on imported books. Even our Bibles and Testaments were, for the most part, printed abroad. The book trade is now one of the greatest branches of business, and many works of standard value and of high reputation in Europe as well as at home have been produced by American authors in every department of literary composition.

While the country has been expanding in dimensions, in numbers, and in wealth, the Government has applied a wise forecast in the adoption of measures necessary, when the world shall no longer be at peace, to maintain the national honor, whether by appropriate displays of vigor abroad or by well-adapted means of defense at home. A navy which has so often illustrated our history by heroic achievements, though restrained in peaceful times in its operations to narrow limits, possesses in its admirable elements the means of great and sudden expansion, and is justly looked upon by the nation as the right arm of its power, an army, still smaller, but not less perfect in its detail, which has on many a field exhibited the military aptitudes and prowess of the race, and demonstrated the wisdom which has presided over its organization and government.

While the gradual and slow enlargement of these respective military arms has been regulated by a jealous watchfulness over the public treasure, there has, nevertheless, been freely given all that was needed to perfect their quality; and each affords the nucleus of any enlargement that the public exigencies may demand, from the millions of brave hearts and strong arms upon the land and water.

The Navy is the active and aggressive element of national defense, and, let loose from our own seacoast, must display its power in the seas and channels of the enemy. To do this it need not be large, and it can never be large enough to defend by its presence at home all our ports and harbors. But, in the absence of the Navy, what can the brave hearts and strong arms of the Army and militia do against the enemy's line-of-battle ships and steamers falling without notice upon our coast? What will guard our cities from tribute, our merchant vessels and our navy-yards from conflagration? Here, again, we see a wise forecast in the system of defensive measures which, especially since the close of the war with Great Britain, has been steadily followed by our Government. While the perils from which our great establishments had just escaped were yet fresh of remembrance, a system of fortifications was begun which now, though not quite complete, fences in our important points with impassable strength. More than four thousand cannon may at any moment, within strong and permanent works, arranged with all the advantages and appliances that the art affords, be turned to the protection of the seacoast and be served by the men whose hearths they shelter. Happy for us that it is so, since these are means of security that time alone can supply; and since the improvements of maritime warfare, by making distant expeditions easy and speedy, have made them more probable and at the same time more difficult to anticipate and provide against. The cost of fortifying all the important points on our whole Atlantic and Gulf of Mexico frontier will not exceed the amount expended on the fortifications of Paris.

In this connection one most important facility in the defense of the country is not to be overlooked; it is the almost instantaneous rapidity with which the soldiers of the Army and any number of the militia corps may be brought to any point where a hostile attack may at any time be made or threatened.

And this extension of territory embraced within the United States, increase of its population, commerce, and manufactures, development of its resources by canals and railroads, and rapidity of intercommunication by innumerable steamboats and telegraphs has been accomplished without the overthrow of or danger to the public liberties by any assumption of military power, and, indeed, without any permanent increase of the Army except for the purpose of frontier defense, and of affording a slight guard to the public property; or of the Navy any further than to assure the navigator that in whatsoever sea he shall sail his ship he is protected by the Stars and Stripes of his country. All this has been done without the shedding of a drop of blood for treason or rebellion; all this while systems of popular representation have regularly been supported in the State governments and in the General Government; all this while laws, National and State, of such a character have been passed and have been so wisely administered that I may stand up here to-day and declare, as I now do declare, in the face of all the intelligent of the age, that for the period which has elapsed from the day that WASHINGTON laid the foundation of this Capitol to the present time there has been no country upon the earth in which life, liberty, and property have been more amply and steadily secured or more freely enjoyed than in these United States of America. Who is there that will deny this? Who is there prepared with a greater or a better example? Who is there that can stand upon the foundation of facts, acknowledged or proved, and assert that these our republican institutions have not answered the true ends of Government beyond all precedent in human history?

There is yet another view. There are still higher considerations. Man is an intellectual being, destined to immortality. There is a spirit in him, and the breath of the Almighty hath given him understanding. Then only is he tending toward his own destiny while he seeks for knowledge or virtue, for the will of his Maker, and for just conceptions of his own duty. Of all important questions, therefore, let this, the most important of all, be first asked and first answered: In what country of the habitable globe of great extent and large population are the means of knowledge most generally diffused and enjoyed among the people? This question admits of one and only one answer. It is here; it is here in these United States. It is among the descendants of those who settled at Jamestown; of those who were pilgrims on the shore of Plymouth, and of those other races of men who in subsequent times have become joined in this great American family. Let one fact incapable of doubt or dispute satisfy every mind on this point. The population of the United States is twenty-three millions. Now take the map of the continent of Europe and spread it out before you. Take your scale and your dividers and lay off in one area, in any shape you please, a triangle, square, circle, parallelogram, or trapezoid, and of an extent that shall contain one hundred and fifty millions of people, and there will be found within the United States more persons who do habitually read and write than can be embraced within the lines of your demarcation.

But there is something more even than this. Man is not only an intellectual but he is also a religious being, and his religious feelings and habits require cultivation.

Let the religious element in man's nature be neglected, let him be influenced by no higher motives than low self-interest and subjected to no stronger restraint than the limits of civil authority, and he becomes the creature of selfish passions or blind fanaticism.

The spectacle of a nation powerful and enlightened, but without Christian faith, has been presented almost within our own day as a warning beacon for the nations.

On the other hand, the cultivation of the religious sentiment represses licentiousness, incites to a general benevolence and the practical acknowledgment of the brotherhood of man, inspires respect for law and order, and gives strength to the whole social fabric, at the same time that it conducts the human soul upward to the Author of its being.

Now, I think it may be stated with truth that in no country in proportion to its population are there so many benevolent establishments connected with religious instruction—Bible, missionary, and tract societies, supported by public and private contributions—as in our own. There are also institutions for the education of the blind, the deaf and dumb; of idiots; for the reception of orphan and destitute children; for moral reform, designed for children and females, respectively; institutions for the reformation of criminals; not to speak of those numerous establishments in almost every county and town in the United States for the reception of the aged, infirm, and destitute poor, many of whom have fled to our shores to escape the poverty and wretchedness of their condition at home.

In the United States there is no church establishment or ecclesiastical authority founded by Government. Public worship is maintained either by voluntary associations and contributions or by trusts and donations of a charitable origin.

Now, I think it safe to say that a greater proportion of the people of the United States attend public worship, decently clad, well behaved, and well seated, than of any other country of the civilized world.

Edifices of religion are seen everywhere. Their aggregate cost would amount to an immense sum of money. They are, in general, kept in good repair and consecrated to the purposes of public worship. In these edifices the people regularly assemble on the Sabbath day, which is sacredly set apart for rest by all classes from secular employment and for religious meditation and worship, to listen to the reading of the Holy Scriptures and discourses from pious ministers of the several denominations.

This attention to the wants of the intellect and of the soul, as manifested by the voluntary support of schools and colleges, of churches and benevolent institutions, is one of the most remarkable characteristics of the American people, not less strikingly exhibited in the new than in the older settlements of the country.

On the spot where the first trees of the forest are felled, near the log cabins of the pioneers, are to be seen rising together the church and the schoolhouse. So has it been from the beginning, and God grant that it may thus continue!

> On other shores, above their moldering towns,
> In sullen pomp, the tall cathedral frowns;
> Simple and frail, our lowly temples throw
> Their slender shadows on the paths below;
> Scarce steals the wind that sweeps the woodland track.
> The larch's perfume from the settler's ax,
> Ere, like a vision of the morning air,
> His slight-framed steeple marks the house of prayer.
> *   *   *   *   *
> Yet Faith's pure hymn beneath its shelter rude
> Breathes out as sweetly to the tangled wood
> As where the rays through blazing oriels pour
> On marble shaft and tessellated floor.

Who does not admit that this unparalleled growth of prosperity and renown is the result, under Providence, of the Union of these States under a general Constitution which guarantees to each State a republican form of government and to every man the enjoyment of life, liberty, and the pursuit of happiness, free from civil tyranny or ecclesiastical domination?

To bring home this idea to the present occasion, who does not feel that when President WASHINGTON laid his hand on the foundation of the first Capitol building he performed a great work of perpetuation of the Union and the Constitution? Who does not feel that this seat of the General Government, healthful in its situation, central in its position, near the mountains from whence gush fresh springs of wonderful virtue, teeming with nature's richest products, and yet not far from the bays and the great estuaries of the sea, easily accessible and generally agreeable in climate and association, does give strength to the Union of these States; that this city, bearing an immortal name, with its broad streets and avenues, its public squares and magnificent edifices of the General Government, erected for the purposes of carrying on within them the important business of the several Departments; for the reception of wonderful and curious inventions, the preservation of the records of American learning and genius, of extensive collections of the products of nature and art, brought hither for study and comparison from all parts of the world; adorned with numerous churches, and sprinkled over, I am happy to say, with many public schools, where all children of the city, without distinction, are provided with the means of obtaining a good education; where there are academies and colleges, professional schools and public libraries, should continue to receive, as it has heretofore received, the fostering care of Congress, and should be regarded as the permanent seat of the National Government? Here, too, a citizen of the great republic of letters, a republic which knows not the metes and bounds of political geography, has indicated prophetically his conviction that America is to exercise a wide and powerful influence in the intellectual world, and therefore has founded in this city, as a commanding position in the field of science and literature, and has placed under the guardianship of the Government, an institution " for the increase and diffusion of knowledge among men."

With each succeeding year new interest is added to the spot. It becomes connected with all the historical associations of our country, with her statesmen and her orators, and, alas! its cemetery is annually enriched with the ashes of her chosen sons.

Before us is the broad and beautiful river, separating two of the thirteen original States, and which a late President, a man of determined purpose and inflexible will, but patriotic heart, desired to span with arches of ever-enduring granite, symbolical of the firmly cemented union of the North and the South. That President was General JACKSON.

On its banks repose the ashes of the Father of his Country, and at one side, by a singular felicity of position, overlooking the city which he designed and which bears his name, rises to his memory the marble column, sublime in its simple grandeur and fitly intended to reach a loftier height than any similar structure on the surface of the whole earth.

Let the votive offerings of his grateful countrymen be freely contributed to carry higher and still higher this monument. May I say, as on another occasion, "Let it rise; let it rise till it meet the sun in his coming; let the earliest light of the morning gild it, and parting day linger and play on its summit!"

Fellow-citizens, what contemplations are awakened in our minds as we assemble here to reenact a scene like that performed by WASHINGTON! Methinks I see his venerable form now before me as presented in the glorious statue by HOUDON, now in the capital of Virginia. He is dignified and grave; but concern and anxiety seem to soften the lineaments of his countenance. The Government over which he presides is yet in the crisis of experiment. Not free from troubles at home, he sees the world in commotion and in arms all around him. He sees that imposing foreign powers are half disposed to try the strength of the recently established American Government. We perceive that mighty thoughts, mingled with fears as well as with hopes, are struggling within him. He heads a short procession over these, the naked fields; he crosses yonder stream on a fallen tree; he ascends to the top of this eminence, whose original oaks of the forest stand as thick around him as if the spot had been devoted to Druidical worship, and here he performs the appointed duty of the day.

And now, fellow-citizens, if this vision were a reality; if WASHINGTON were now actually among us, and if he could draw around him the shades of the great public men of his own days, patriots and warriors, orators and statesmen, and were to address us in their presence, would he not say to us, " Ye men of this generation, I rejoice and thank God for being able to see that our labors and toils and sacrifices were not in vain. You are prosperous, you are happy, you are grateful. The fire of liberty burns brightly and steadily in your hearts, while DUTY and the LAW restrain it from bursting forth in wild and destructive conflagration. Cherish liberty, as you love it; cherish its securities, as you wish to preserve it; maintain the Constitution which we labored so painfully to establish, and which has been to you such a source of inestimable blessings; preserve the Union of the States, cemented as it was by our prayers, our tears, and our blood; be true to God, to your country, and to your duty. So shall the whole Eastern World follow the morning sun to contemplate you as a nation; so shall all succeeding generations honor you as they honored us, and so shall that Almighty Power, which so graciously protected us and which now protects you, shower its everlasting blessings upon you and your posterity."

Great father of your country! we heed your words; we feel their force as if you now uttered them with life of flesh and blood. Your example teaches us, your public life teaches us your sense of the value of the blessings of the Union. Those blessings our fathers have tasted, and we have tasted, and still taste. Nor do we intend that those who come after us shall be denied the same high fruition. Our honor as well as our happiness is concerned. We can not, we dare not, we will not betray our sacred trust. We will not filch from posterity the treasure placed in our hands to be transmitted to other generations. The bow that gilds the cloud in the heavens, the pillars that uphold the firmament, may disappear and fall away in the hour appointed by the will of God, but until that day comes or so long as our lives may last no ruthless hand shall undermine that bright arch of Union and Liberty which spans the continent from Washington to California.

Fellow-citizens, we must sometimes be tolerant to folly and patient at the sight of the extreme waywardness of men; but I confess that when I reflect on the renown of our past history, on our present prosperity and greatness, and on what the future hath yet to unfold, and when I see that there are men who can find in all this nothing good, nothing valuable, nothing truly glorious, I feel that all their reason has fled from them and left the entire control over their judgment and their actions to insane folly and fanaticism, and, more than all, fellow-citizens, if the purposes of fanatics and disunionists should be accomplished, the patriotic and intelligent of our generation would seek to hide themselves from the scorn of the world and go about to find dishonorable graves.

Fellow-citizens, take *courage; be of good cheer*. We shall come to no such ignoble end. We shall live and not die. During the period allotted to our several lives we shall continue to rejoice in the return of this anniversary. The ill-omened sounds of fanaticism will be hushed; the ghostly specters of *Secession* and *Disunion* will disappear, and the enemies of united constitutional liberty, if their hatred can not be appeased, may prepare to sear their eyeballs as they behold the steady flight of the AMERICAN EAGLE on his burnished wings for years and years to come.

President FILLMORE, it is your singularly good fortune to perform an act such as that which the earliest of your predecessors performed fifty-eight years ago. You stand where he stood. You lay your hand on the corner stone of a building designed greatly to extend that whose corner stone he laid. Changed, changed is everything around. The same sun, indeed, shone upon his head which now shines upon yours. The same broad river rolled at his feet and bathes his last resting place that now rolls at yours. But the site of this city was then mainly an open field. Streets and avenues have since been laid out and completed, squares and public grounds inclosed and ornamented, until the city which bears his name, although comparatively inconsiderate in numbers and wealth, has become quite fit to be the seat of government of a great and united people.

Sir, may the consequences of the duty which you perform so auspiciously to-day equal those which flowed from his act. Nor this only; may the principles of your administration and the wisdom of your political conduct be such as that the world of the present day and all history hereafter may be at no loss to perceive what example you have made your study.

Fellow-citizens, I now bring this address to a close by expressing to you, in the words of the great Roman orator, the deepest wish of my heart, and which I know deeply penetrates the hearts of all who hear me: " Duo modo, hæc opto; unum, UT MORIENS POPULUM ROMANUM LIBERUM RELINQUAM; hoc mihi majus a diis immortalibus dari nihil potest: alterum, ut ita cuique eveniat, ut de republica quisque mereatur."

And now, fellow-citizens, with hearts void of hatred, envy, and malice toward our countrymen, or any of

them, or toward the subjects or citizens of other Governments, or toward any member of the great family of man, but exulting, nevertheless, in our own peace, security, and happiness, in the grateful recollection of the past, and in the glorious hopes of the future, let us return to our homes and with all humiliation and devotion offer our thanks to the Father of all our mercies, political, social, and religious.

This concluded the exercises at the Capitol, a salute of artillery being fired from the battery on the public reservation at the north end of the Capitol, and the civil and military associations returned in excellent order to their respective places of rendezvous, where they were dismissed.

The celebration of the day closed with a display of fireworks from the Mall south of the President's house.

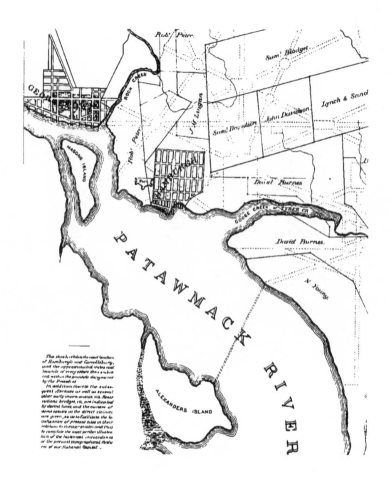

Rob.ᵗ Peter.

Sam.ˡ Blodget

GEO...

ROCK CREEK

Lynch & Sand

Sam.ˡ Davidson

John Davidson

J. M. Lingan

Rob.ᵗ Peter

MASONS ISLAND

LUDLOW...OWN

David Burnes

GOOSE CREEK ... TYBER CR.

PATAWMACK RIVER

David Burnes.

N. Young.

This sketch exhibits the exact location
of Hamburgh and Carrollsburg,
and the approximated extent and
bounds of every estate then subscri-
bed within the presents designated
by the President.
In addition thereto the subsequent Avenues as well as several
other early improvements, viz. Reservations bridges, etc, are indicated
by dotted lines, and the owners of
same estates in the direct vicinity
are given, so as to facilitate the lo-
calisation of present sites in their
relation to river estates and thus
to complete the most perfect illustra-
tion of the historical antecedents
of the present topographical features of our National Capital.

ALEXANDERS ISLAND

SKETCH
OF
WASHINGTON IN EMBRYO,
VIZ
Previous to its Survey by Major L'ENFANT.
1792.
Compiled from the rare historical researches
of
Dᴿ JOSEPH M. TONER,
who by special favor has permitted the use of his labor and material's
for the publication of a grand historical map of this District
now in progress by his efforts combined with the skill of
S. R. SEIBERT C.E.
1874.

1893.

PUBLISHED BY AUTHORITY OF THE
CAPITOL CENTENNIAL COMMITTEE.

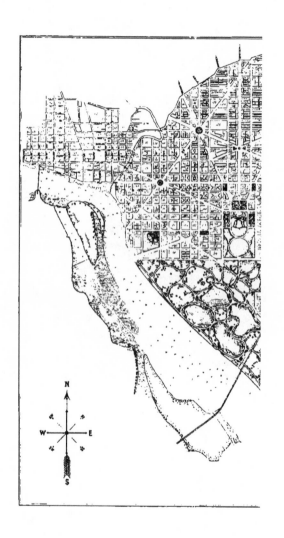

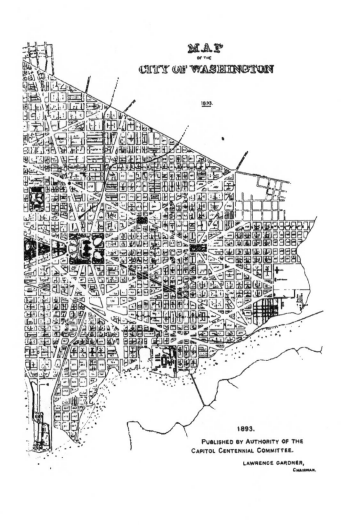

MAP
OF THE
CITY OF WASHINGTON

1893.

1893.
PUBLISHED BY AUTHORITY OF THE
CAPITOL CENTENNIAL COMMITTEE.

LAWRENCE GARDNER,
CHAIRMAN.

CPSIA information can be obtained
at www.ICGtesting.com
Printed in the USA
BVHW071325190819
556214BV00006B/749/P